TWAYNE'S WORLD AUTHORS SERIES

A Survey of the World's Literature

Sylvia E. Bowman, Indiana University
GENERAL EDITOR

SOUTH AFRICA

EDITOR

JOSEPH JONES, UNIVERSITY OF TEXAS AT AUSTIN

Ezekiel Mphahlele

TWAS 417

Ezekiel Mphahlele

EZEKIEL MPHAHLELE

By URSULA A. BARNETT

TWAYNE PUBLISHERS
A DIVISION OF G. K. HALL & CO., BOSTON

Library of Congress Cataloging in Publication Data

Barnett, Ursula A
  Ezekiel Mphahlele.

  (Twayne's world authors series ; TWAS 417 : South
Africa)
  Bibliography: p. 187 - 90.
  Includes index.
  1. Mphahlele, Ezekiel.
PR 9369.3. M67Z6   823   76-18881
ISBN 0-8057-6257-4

For Hyman

Contents

About the Author

Ursula A. Barnett received her Ph.D. from the University of Cape Town for a historical study of black Southern African literature in the English language. Born in Yugoslavia and educated in Germany, England, South Africa and the United States (Columbia University Graduate School of Journalism), she is presently managing editor of a literary agency in Cape Town. She has published a number of critical essays about South African writing in journals in the United States, and has contributed to a book of essays on English language and literature in South Africa, published in Cape Town. Her revised dissertation is to be published in English in Holland shortly. Dr. Barnett has been active in promoting better English teaching in black South African schools. She is married and has three children.

Preface

In 1945 a small group of black intellectuals met in the Ghandi Hall, Johannesburg, to form a black cultural unity movement. Speakers stressed the need for black intellectuals to create an impression on the contemporary world and thus attract world attention to their sufferings, aspirations, and ideals. The movement was short-lived. The following year the African Bookman, a small publishing house in Cape Town, which produced books for black readers, printed seven hundred copies of a slim volume of short stories, *Man Must Live*, by a twenty-six-year-old high school teacher, Ezekiel Mphahlele. These stories were not designed to protest against the conditions under which the black man lived in South Africa, and seven hundred copies could hardly be expected to make an impact. Yet they drew attention, as one reviewer put it, to an astounding world, one of which the white South African was almost totally ignorant.

Neither cultural meetings nor isolated work of an aspiring writer provided sufficient impetus to start a literature for the urban black man in South Africa. He had been living in the cities for two or three generations, he had largely lost his tribal affiliations, and he wanted a Western-style education. He still spoke the vernacular at home, but he wanted his education and his reading matter in English. The English language opened a new world for him in which he could at least dream of enjoying the comforts and the power of the white population.

The answer to his literary requirements came from an unexpected quarter. In 1950 a magazine for black readers appeared entitled *African Drum*. It was founded by the son of a white South African millionaire, Jim Bailey, as a business proposition. *Drum*, as it came to be called, was popular and brash and catered mainly to the less sophisticated strata of black society. However, it was often fearless in its support of black interests and exposure of injustices, and it gave an opportunity, however grudgingly, to black writers. A whole spate of black talent, which had never had an opening before, began to break into print. Ezekiel Mphahlele eventually joined its staff and became its fiction editor.

His stories for *Drum* centered around the life of black South Africans in the township outside Johannesburg and Pretoria. He wrote of the despair and hopes of black people and gave a vivid account of their daily lives.

Although Mphahlele spoke his mother tongue, Northern Sesotho, at home and on the streets and learned English seriously only at the age of thirteen, he, like his contemporaries in Johannesburg, wrote only in English. All his reading was in English, and his love for English literature developed at an early age. On the salary of a domestic servant, his mother struggled to give him a good education, and by his own efforts he completed it when he gained a Ph.D. degree in English literature.

Mphahlele once explained, at a conference he chaired in Sweden[1] where the language African writers should use came under discussion, that when a writer feels the creative impulse kick him in the pit of his stomach, he pours himself out in the medium that comes to him naturally. For him it was obviously English. His early works contained errors, but they are negligible when we consider the vitality of his writing, which gains from the jargon of black township speech.

When short stories were no longer able to express all that the black writers had to say, they turned to autobiography, and again Mphahlele was in the forefront. His autobiography, *Down Second Avenue*,[2] was the first to appear. It was an immediate success.

By the time it was published, however, Mphahlele had left his country. He had been banned from teaching for campaigning against a new education act which threatened to bring the black child separate and inferior education; and he hated journalism. He felt stifled in the South African atmosphere and thus decided to go into voluntary exile. His subsequent writing, published and written abroad, eventually suffered from severance from the source of its lifeblood. The longer he stayed away, the less convincingly could he write about the life and people he had known intimately. For a time he turned mainly to the writing of essays and critical surveys, and became a highly respected authority on African literature.

Not long after he left South Africa, Mphahlele was named by the Government as a writer who may not be quoted and whose writing

Preface

may not be disseminated in South Africa, in terms of the Suppression
of Communism Act. Thus his work may no longer be read in his own
country. Nevertheless, in his interests and in the subject matter of
most of his writing, Mphahlele remains a South African writer,
biding his time like many others, until he can return and continue
his career as a teacher, a critic, and a creative writer about and for
the black people of South Africa.

Mphahlele has been closely associated with every phase of black
South African literature and often gave it direction or led the way.
After two novels — one yet to be published at the time of writing —
he has recently turned to poetry. The story of his life is almost inex-
tricably interwoven with his writing and we shall thus study both
simultaneously.

I would like to thank Mr. Mphahlele for his never-failing help and
his patience with my many questions about his life and works. My
thanks also go to his sister, Mrs. Tabitha, and to Mr. Dickson Mphahlele for their help.

I wish to thank the following publishers, agents, and individuals
for permission to quote from their works: Mr. J. Rollnick, formerly of
African Bookman (*Man Must Live*); Messrs. J. Farquharson (Peter
Abrahams); Collins Publishers (Anthony Sampson: *Drum*); East
African Publishing House (*In Corner B*); Societé Nouvelle Presence
Africaine ("Negro Culture in Africa") *Studies in Black Literature*
(Interview with E. M.); Macmillan Publishing Co. (*The Wanderers*);
Doubleday (*Down Second Avenue*); Mr. E. Mphahlele (Manuscript
of "Chirundu"); Messrs. Praeger and Faber & Faber (*The African
Image*).

Ursula A. Barnett

Cape Town
U. A. B.
August, 1975

Chronology

1919   Ezekiel Mphahlele born in Marabastad township, Pretoria, South Africa.
1924   Sent to live with his grandmother in Maupaneng in North-eastern Transvaal.
1932   Returns to Marabastad.
1935   Enters St. Peter's Secondary School, Johannesburg.
1939   Enters Adams Teachers Training College, Natal.
1941   Works at an institution for the blind. Continues private studies for matriculation.
1945   Joins staff of Orlando High School, Johannesburg, as Afrikaans and English master. Marries Rebecca Mochadibane.
1946   Publication of *Man Must Live*.
1947   Birth of first son, Anthony.
1949   Gains degree of Bachelor of Arts, University of South Africa.
1950   Birth of daughter, Teresa Kefilwe.
1952   Banned from teaching at South African government schools.
1953   Birth of daughter, Motswiri.
1954   Brief period as teacher in Basutoland. Returns to Johannesburg. Teaches at St. Peter's Secondary School. Gains degree of Bachelor of Arts, Honors, University of South Africa.
1955   Joins staff of *Drum*.
1956   Gains degree of Master of Arts, University of South Africa.
1956 -   Short stories appear in *Drum*.
1957
1957   Literary editor of *Drum*. (September) Leaves South Africa for Nigeria. Lecturer at University of Ibadan.
1959   Publication of *Down Second Avenue*. Long leave spent in Britain. Birth of son, Chabi Robert.
1961   Publication of *The Living and the Dead*. Birth of daughter, Puso. Banning order gazetted.

1961   Resident in Paris as head of African Program of Congress for
1963   Cultural Freedom.
1962   Publication of *African Image*.
1963   Resident in Nairobi, Kenya. Founds Mbari cultural institu-
        tion.
1966   Joins staff of Denver University as professor of English.
1967   Publication of *In Corner B*.
1968   Gains degree of Doctor of Philosophy, University of Den-
        ver. Joins staff of University of Zambia at Lusaka as pro-
        fessor of English.
1970   Returns to Denver University.
1971   Publication of *The Wanderers*.
1972   Publication of *Voices in the Whirlwind and Other Essays*.
1973   Publication of *African Image*, revised edition.
1974   Joins staff of University of Pennsylvania in Philadelphia as
        full professor of English.

CHAPTER 1

Man Must Live

I The Tribe

AFTER conquering Zulu chief Mzilikazi had subjugated the Pedi group of the Transvaal Sotho people early in the nineteenth century, a small Pedi tribe, the Mphahlele, helped the chief to reestablish his ascendancy. From that time onward, as a sign of gratitude, the men of the chief's clan usually took their chief wives from the Mphahlele tribe. There is still a village named Mphahlele in Sekhukhuneland, an area in the Transvaal bounded on the northwest and the west by the Oliphant River and on the east by the Steelport River. After crushing defeats, first by the Boers and then by the British, Sekhukhuneland was reserved for "Bantu" (i.e., tribal black) occupation to the exclusion of other races. Today, under the South African government's "homelands" policy, eventual independence is envisaged for the ethnic group of the area.

The country is mountainous, consisting of a complex system of conical mountains, dark in color, with many deep valleys between. The Pedi are of Sotho stock, the name being derived from a word meaning "black people." Their origin is unknown but it is thought likely that they emigrated southward from the region of the Great Lakes in Central Africa.

Education has been of great importance in the Mphahlele tribe ever since contact with Europeans. Mphahlele had the first registered tribal school in the Transvaal early in the century. The chief at the time, having matriculated at Lovedale College in the Cape, was the most highly educated chief in the area. Many of the younger members of the tribe turned to teaching.

Ezekiel Mphahlele was born in 1919 in Pretoria. His father, Moses, a cousin of the chief, had, like many young men, left the village to seek his fortune in the city. There he had met Eva Mogale,

also of the Pedi group, who came from the Lydenburg district where
her father had been a cobbler and a minister of the Lutheran church.
When Ezekiel was five, however, he and his younger brother and
sister were sent back to the northeastern Transvaal, to the little
village of Maupaneng, which nestled against the dark woody mountains. There he lived with his paternal grandmother for the next
eight years.

Mphahlele's origin is of deep concern to the student of his writing,
especially in view of the contention of his critics many years later
that his social and educational background was a purely Western urban one. Mphahlele regards the policy of the South African government which promises independence to the various ethnic groups in
South Africa as one of the most pernicious manifestations of
apartheid, an attempt to force the black man back to his tribal
origins, in order both to destroy black nationalism and to deprive the
black man of equal status as a citizen in the country of his birth. His
concern, however, is less with the political than with the cultural
aspect. Culture, for him, is always a movement forward, never a
movement back. In an address to the Second Congress of Negro
Writers and Artists in Rome[1] he said:

South African White has come to accept a double stream of cultural life,
which the African hates because he knows that he can never be independent
even in the dream-state the white man fraudulently says he can create for
the Black man. . . Traditional culture, much of which the missionary
destroyed, has come to be associated by the Negro with an inferior political
status and ethnic grouping which will destroy all the work that has been
done by the educated Negro to forge a Black nationalism.[2]

II *Childhood*

It is for this reason that Mphahlele tends to gloss over his ethnic
roots. He refuses to romanticize his past, either racially or personally.
He describes the village where he spent his early years as a rural
slum. His early childhood is symbolized in his autobiographical
writing by his paternal grandmother, unsmiling, sitting "under a
small lemon tree next to the hut, as big as fate, as forbidding as a
mountain, stern as a mimosa tree." He continues: "Things stand out
clearly in my mind from those years: my granny, the mountain on
the foot of which the village clung like a leech, and the mountain
darkness, so solid and dense. And my granny seemed to conspire
with the mountain and the dark to frighten us."[3]

The terror which the dark tropical mountains and the raging rivers inspired in the lonely, ragged, vermin-ridden herd-boy, while he hunted for lost cattle, appears to have pursued Mphahlele in nightmares all his life. When his mother came to fetch the children eight years later and took them back to Pretoria, he had come home.

Home was Marabastad, a typical slum area in the Pretoria district. While today black people are grouped strictly in separate locations, the Marabastad of the 1920's and 1930's housed black people of all shades and ethnic origins. They were mainly Southern Sotho, but there were also many other groups, including Indians and people of mixed blood.

His mother, Mphahlele tells us, owed allegiance to tribal authority only in a detached academic way. The only features that identified her with the tribe were the language and the behavior patterns they still upheld at home.

While he spoke Northern Sotho at home, the language of communication with most of his neighbors was a mixture of Southern Sotho and Afrikaans. His medium of instruction, right from the beginning, at the Methodist church school he attended, was English, and his own reading in English began early. As soon as he could read, he devoured comics and any books which he could find. "It became a mania with me," he says, "I couldn't let printed matter pass." He felt inferior to the children in his class when he arrived from the country. "I was pretty poor in English . . . I read and read, till it hurt."[4] His first earnings were in the form of tickets to the movies, received from boys who wanted him to read the captions for silent films.

His mother spoke English with ease. Very early he saw the necessity for being proficient in English. It was "a key to job opportunities" and it gave him "a sense of power to be able to master the external world which came to us in English," he tells us and explains that films, household furniture, advertising, and "printed forms that regulate some of the mechanics of living and dying" all came in English. Students and teachers recognized this and developed a love for English as a result. "A love that *had* to be self-generated, given all the hostile external factors."[5]

III   *Man Must Live*

Mphahlele's first collection of short stories was published in 1946. By this time he was teaching in a high school in the Orlando township in Johannesburg, a position he had reached through his own tenacity and persistence, and with the encouragement of his mother. "You must go to college, my son, and come and look after me and your brother and your sister. They must also go to school,"[6] she said to him. His maternal grandmother, with whom the children lived after the father deserted them, took in white people's washing and one of her daughters contributed to the family funds by illegally brewing beer. Two sons were sent to board at a teacher's training college, while a third awaited his turn. Ezekiel's mother, from her earnings of £ 3 a month as a domestic servant, sent him to St. Peter's Secondary School, a high school run by the Community of the Resurrection. It cost her £ 15 a year. Before his last examination Ezekiel almost suffered a nervous breakdown, knowing that if he failed there would be no money for a further year. He passed easily, however, and, after working as a messenger for a year, he continued his studies at Adams College in Natal, a private mission institution run by the United Congregational Church (American Board). Among students of this college who later achieved honor were Chief Gatsha Buthelezi, Prime Minister of Kwazulu, and Seretse Khama, Prime Minister of Botswana. Nobel prize-winner Chief Albert Luthuli once taught there. Here Mphahlele qualified as a teacher. His first position, however, was that of clerk for an institution for the blind.

During this time he was studying privately for the Matriculation certificate. He was earning £ 12 a month, out of which he had to buy his books, send money to his mother for his brother's and sister's schooling, and clothe himself. When he first became a high school teacher in Orlando township, he earned £13 a month. He was now married. He had met his wife, Rebecca Mochadibane, a student teacher at a Johannesburg training college, when she came with a group of other students to recite and sing to the blind at the institute.

Mphahlele had begun to write short stories in the early 1940's. "Something strange happened to me as I studied by candle light, listening at intervals to the throb of night out there. I found myself writing a short story. I know I had been burning with an urge to say something in writing . . . I had not read any short stories before — of the artful kind we compose today. Lots of tales, yes."[7]

When asked about his early stories recently, Mphahlele said that they were a kind of adventure into the literary field.

I wrote things without the intention of having them published, and when I got them together, I sent them to a small publishing house just as a matter of interest, to see what their attitude would be towards them. . . . It was about 1941 when I started to write them, and things were pretty confused in my mind. I was twenty and was living in a town on the reef — the Johannesburg golden reef, about twelve miles out of Johannesburg, and it was a very secluded place. So I had a good deal of the natural setting around me — I wasn't living in a ghetto.

I was interested in people, in their own ghetto life and their own little dramas and tragedies, which would not necessarily have to do with the racial issue. That was my first entry into literature — my interest in people as people and not as political victims.[8]

In his autobiography, *Down Second Avenue,* he tells us: "In 1945 I sent ten [short stories] to the African Bookman in Cape Town which had ventured into producing monographs and pamphlets by Africans on political and social subjects. The publisher wrote back to say he wanted to publish five of the stories, adding that he was taking a chance as he had never handled fiction of any kind before. In 1947 [sic] the final product was sent to me; a neat little volume with pen drawings for illustrations, under the title *Man Must Live*"[9]

Although the characters in the stories are not as yet realistic portraits of the earthy people among whom he lived, *Man Must Live* already sets the pattern for Mphahlele's future writing in its dependence on personal experience. It is tempting in all Mphahlele's writing to spot the corresponding incident or character in his life, but this can obviously serve no useful purpose except to demonstrate authenticity. Thus, in "Out Brief Candle," the boy Sello, like the young Mphahlele, works as a messenger in a solicitor's office. "Tomorrow You Shall Reap" is written in the first person and the setting is the Pietersburg of Mphahlele's early days.

It is the mental, rather than the factual experience, however, that constitutes the material for his writing. "Whatever I write," he tells us, "will always be rooted in my boyhood experiences."[10] These experiences, he says, helped to define his responses to life wherever he lived. This he calls the "tyranny of place," but a tyranny "that gives me the base to write, the very reason to write."[11]

Stephen, the narrator of "Tomorrow You Shall Reap," like Ezekiel, is the child of parents who constantly quarrel. In this story the father leaves the mother because she bore him only one child. The mother goes insane, sets fire to the grass, and burns to death. Mphahlele's father threw a pot of burning stew at his mother. When she returned from the hospital she laid a charge against him. He was found guilty and sentenced to fourteen days' imprisonment with the option of a fine. He paid the fine, and that was the last time Ezekiel saw his father. There is no doubt that the boy Stephen is speaking for the young Ezekiel when he says: "Yet, I told myself, I must not think of it. I must think of a new life at a boarding-school. I must not pity myself even if circumstances seem to justify self-pity. I must try to run away from my conscious self and dope myself with romantic ideas and ambitions so that I should not feel the pain of blunt reality."[12] In the fictional version the boy meets his father again; blind and repentant, he has reaped the wages of his sin.

Like Ezekiel, Stephen spent his early years in the country as a herd-boy, but it is not the country as Mphahlele later writes about it. Here birds whistle, doves coo, and cattle low. The river has sparkling waters that are sweet and pure. The mountains may be fearful in appearance but they give him shelter under their huge crags. The young boy is free to wander over the vast stretch of low veld country, thickly grown with mimosa bush "that has a dignity all its own." Nostalgically he recalls:

What delicious gum those mimosa trees afforded! Man and baboon were fellow-guests here. The "marula" trees stood defiantly as if reaching out for the sky. I recalled the seasons when wild fruits were ripe; how we used to curdle milk in the peels of "marula" fruit with its juice or "moshidi" juice. The taste hereof can drive a man to hug the stem of the tree in selfish adoration of the sweetness that Nature can harbour in this tree. As if we were not content with what the "marula" tree gave us, we used to drive goats to eat the fruit from the ground. They would chew their cud overnight, during which the stones of the fruit dropped out of the mouth. Taste of the nuts therein, reader, and you have another wonder in the kingdom of sweetness.[13]

It seems likely that as the circumstances of Mphahlele's life became increasingly bitter, so the scenery of his early childhood grew darker for him, denser and more confined.

In these stories, as in his later fiction, Mphahlele often identifies with the chief characters and shares their thoughts and feelings. "The Leaves were Falling" represents a poignant mental experience. The Reverend Katsane Melato has lost the confidence of his congregation for following an unpopular line of action. He lies on a heap of leaves, and the leaves appear to say to him:

You see, it's this way: You take up a career to be of service to your people. Perhaps you get on well at first. Then something comes up, and when you think you have them in your hand they slip out like quicksilver. You chase after them, but all the time you seem to run either slower than they or at the same pace. . . .

Each one has a kingdom of his own, a little paradise of his own — his self. He wants to rule over it. When he thinks he is king over his little world he imagines he can widen his territory to include other little worlds of self. So here you are, Katsane. . . . Perhaps the sting of need for sleep and comfort in your slum life has made you wonder where to draw the line between good and evil. . . . You have felt some evil power somewhere must be crushed, and you set out to do it.[14]

This story was written some fifteen to twenty years before Mphahlele left South Africa and began his wanderings, but the restlessness is already there. Here Katsane continues:

You distrust mankind and find yourself distrusting your own self — of the same species. You are an exile. You know not where you are going. . . . Are you seeking a paradise Katsane? Do you want to be at peace with your conscience? Are you denying the very substance that made you? No, you wouldn't know, of course — that is the true though painful thing. There lies the sting! Who would know what he really wants on this earth. Ha, ha! Here man and animal are not different, even though he would like to think he is! Again, there is the blunt and painful fact. Oh, Katsane, you are so weak, so weak . . . oh, so weak. . . .[15]

The Reverend Katsane's dilemma is that of the African intellectual at the time of Mphahlele's youth. In a society where all black people live together in ghettos and are deprived of the intellectual amenities of the larger society, there is little class distinction based on education and intellect. Thus the people among whom he lived expected a great deal from teachers like Mphahlele and clergymen like Katsane. Having helped such chosen ones attain the intellectual level of the white man, they looked forward to being lifted, themselves, to a better life and to having political and financial power procured for them. Yet the teacher earned little more than the unskilled laborer, and the ghetto walls remained as solid as ever. The people became disillusioned. "It is a lonely man," Mphahlele tells us, "who is not taken seriously by his own people, yet cannot keep aloof from them and their daily miseries."[16]

The Reverend Katsane Melato and Zungu in "Man Must Live," like Ezekiel, must cope with their responsibilities. They enclose themselves in a shell of stubbornness to hide their lack of confidence, and in due course they learn their lesson that life must continue "for good or for bad, tomorrow and tomorrow and on forever."[17]

IV   *The Stories*

Zungu, the hero of "Man Must Live," makes a cult of the philosophy of survival to replace the ethics more acceptable to the world around him: "Let men accuse, deride and ridicule you in your actions; let them complain that you don't respect or fear them; let them say you don't earn your living honestly; but they too, sooner or later, will come down to the hard, cold and indisputable fact that man must live."[18] Zungu has contempt for those who read a great deal but do not know how to live, and for money-minded people who admittedly wanted, like him, to live, but usually died in pursuit of life long before they started to live.

For Zungu, life is like the magic carpet he had read of in school: "It carried you over mountain peaks, over green valleys and beautiful streams, through fearfully dark gorges and over rugged ugly boulders; over sharp unfriendly briars, through jungles and dark mysterious kingdoms, where you felt you were being swallowed up into the pit of death; and again you could emerge into the smiling world, swim in the fragrant smell of flowers, taste of the sweet, the bitter and the bitter-sweet fruit; always and for ever borne by the magic carpet — whither no one knew. Yet, whatever the end, man must live."[19]

Zungu feels he has reason to be pleased with himself, his work, and his life. He is tall and strong; as a railway policeman, he controls masses of people who are not unlike the sheep and cattle he looked after as a boy in Zululand; and his intelligence is demonstrably greater than theirs. But Zungu's attitude is merely a stance: he is essentially unsure of himself. With the "machine," the railways organization, behind him, he is full of bluster, calling out the names of the stations in his fine baritone voice and directing the two-legged sheep on their way. When he faces a situation as an individual, however, his confidence vanishes. He has not married because he is shy of women, and he cringes before his employers and white people generally. He constantly has to remind himself of his motto; otherwise he becomes overwhelmed with a lack of purpose, a feeling of hollowness, emptiness, and a vague sense of defeat.

To give his life purpose, Zungu feels that he must marry. He woos and wins a wealthy widow whom he had sheltered when she missed her train. He takes life more and more for granted, allowing himself to be borne along. Eventually he stops work and drinks heavily.

Zungu's downfall is due to his misunderstanding of the philosophy he has chosen. Man must live, it is true, but he cannot survive if he underestimates his fellowmen and expects to live at their expense. He also overestimates the power of the "machine," the organization, as an aid to survival.

Zungu's wife and step-children insult him constantly, and he deteriorates rapidly. One day they desert him, and he realizes that they had considered him merely as a tool whose usefulness has ceased. He sets the house on fire, only at the last moment to remember his motto and rush out, in flames. A neighbor saves him. Once out of the hospital, he sets up an iron shack. Understanding has come to him at last. All his life he has clung to the mechanics of living as to a magic carpet. Now, stooping under a burden, mostly drunk and muttering to himself, he still clings to life. We are asked not only to sympathize with but to admire the tenacity with which he adheres to his faith of individual survival, now shorn of the magic of a false superiority.

Mphahlele's characters know, or come to realize, that they must survive, not physically or communally, but spiritually as individuals, by strictly adhering to a moral code. This code is not necessarily identical with the morals accepted by the community in which they live. Courage, for example, does not have to mean facing the common enemy, but rather maintaining the truth as you yourself see it.

This courage is embodied in the Reverend Katsane Melato in "The Leaves Were Falling." The plot of this story has a historical basis. Fees for baptism in the Methodist Church had been raised just at a time when black congregants were resenting white supervision of black churches. One preacher, the Reverend Alfred Mushi, consequently broke away from the Bantu Methodist Church and propagated his revolt against oppression by staging pageants and appealing to the emotion of his audiences. Mphahlele's fictional clergyman, Katsane, while he approves of the principle of protesting against the raised fee, cannot condone this method of fighting for it. His congregation, which had once loved and admired him, turns from him. He leaves them and wanders about the countryside for many days until he collapses and is picked up by the roadside. The only one who has stood by him is the girl Lindi Chimandi. In the hospital he is reunited with Lindi, who has been searching for him.

He asks her to join him, as his wife, in the adventure of life, and she agrees. She still has faith in him as a true leader and shepherd of the people.

Katsane's problem is not a religious or a political one. Like Zungu, he knows that life must be lived, but with his more sophisticated background he also knows that there is no glib phrase to express it:

As he lies bundled there he murmured to himself: "I must hang on . . . but for what god? Where is that god? . . . Are you there? . . . What? . . . Bow down my head to you? . . . Oh, let the devil claim my decaying flesh and bones — this walking drum, — or dust be my end. . . . I must . . . I must . . . I must . . . I. . . ."[20]

As the only leaf left hanging on a drying, sapless twig, he wonders how long he can endure, but it will not matter since leaves always do fall and will continue to do so forever.

This is the only story Mphahlele has written in which a parson is the main character. Another black clergyman in South African fiction is immediately brought to mind, Alan Paton's Reverend Kumalo in *Cry the Beloved Country*, which appeared two years after "The Leaves were Falling." Unlike Katsane, Kumalo never has any difficulty in solving a moral dilemma. There is only one right way and that is the way of God. His moral code is evergreen, and he thus does not have to worry about falling leaves. His is the tragedy of external events.

It was at the time of writing this story that Mphahlele began to have doubts about Christianity. In retrospect he has explained that he rejected the Christian faith because it is alien to African traditions, but at the time his quarrel was rather with organized religion and its lack of comfort to the oppressed. Lindi says: "Some of us can move men with words, but cannot lead them to the goal to which we have moved them. Some of us bang fists on tables, fling catch-phrases at their audiences to lure them, drive panic into them, but fail at organizing confused minds, silently and tactfully."[21] Mphahlele could no longer find any strength in a faith that had no answer to the man-imposed suffering he saw around him.

Sello, in "Out Brief Candle," is a victim of his surroundings, whose will to survive has been corroded by his feelings of choking hatred and revenge. He is a foundling who has never been accepted by his peers. He can fall back neither on the cogwheels of modern living like Zungu, nor on the love and admiration of his community to give him even a false sense of security. He feels that his only hope of survival is renunciation, a state of passivity as in nature. Thus he expresses his regrets that he cannot be as the grass which sways in the wind, taking things as they come. Action to him is not an effort to survive but to destroy. His adoptive mother Annah pampers him, asking nothing in return, and thus fails to act as an anchor. Sello feels that life is senseless; it is just a mad, cruel world, as his mother has taught him. There is no point in continuing. He has his revenge against the boys who have continually tormented him and insulted his mother, when he kills one of them in a sparring match. When the police come for him, he jumps to his death.

In "Tomorrow You Shall Reap" and in "Unwritten Episodes" the theme of survival does not motivate the characters. Rather, there is the conventional moral of virtue rewarded. It seems likely that these stories were written earlier, and it would have been better to exclude them. "Unwritten Episodes" is at times embarrassingly mawkish, and the language is stilted and often incorrect. The plot, in which love conquers all, could appear in a true confession periodical. The heroine, Sylvia Direko, is noted for her "artless deportment" and "frank disposition."[22] She harbors and nurses "a violent contempt and hatred" for the young man who "showed the white feather by deserting her the day she told him of her condition."[23] With "tearful eyes" she leaves the baby at "The Refuge," an institution where there "must be invisible archives . . . containing unwritten records of broken suicidal resolutions and fears to venture out once more into the sea of life."[24] She works as a typist and joins a dramatic society. There she plays Juliet to one Larry Maphoto's Romeo. He is a young man who has lived happily in "his little sheltered world of plenty; the little heaven which knows no despair or bitterness."[25] He is drawn more and more toward Sylvia until his possessive fiancee, Joyce Xaba, becomes suspicious and makes a scene. She knows of Sylvia's past and tells Larry about it, but Larry sympathizes with the girl and tells her of his love. Larry's father feels that his son is betraying the honor and dignity of his class, but Larry is adamant in wishing to marry her, and together they face a new life full of inner hopes of joy and peace.

There is little in this story, or in "Tomorrow You Shall Reap," that points to future creative ability. In the latter, Mphahlele does show some skill in conveying the feeling of simple love between a shy boy and a more sophisticated girl. The plot is even less convincing than that of "Unwritten Episodes," and far more melodramatic. The narrator, Stephen, meets an old classmate, Mariah Makwe, while on

holiday with a friend in the country, and they fall in love. Stephen's
mother, we are told earlier in the story, killed herself as a result of
the father's desertion. The boy is still painfully affected by the
memory, which "gnawed" at his "soul."[26] He meets Mariah's blind
father, Shikwane Makwe, who is inexplicably opposed to a union
between the two young people. The reader realizes, of course,
through Shikwane's muttered asides, that he is Stephen's father.
Stephen and Mariah are saved, however, from having to abandon an
incestuous relationship when the old man tells them on his deathbed
that he and his second wife had adopted Mariah.

Mphahlele has virtually disowned his first collection and never
lists it among his writings. In the epilogue to *Down Second Avenue*
he says: "I can never summon enough courage to read a line from
any of the stories that were published in 1947 under the title *Man
Must Live* again. In ten years my perspective has changed enor-
mously from escapist writing to protest writing and, I hope to
something of a higher order, which is the ironic meeting between
protest and acceptance in their widest terms."[27]

Mphahlele is therefore aware today of the amateurishness and sentimentality of the stories, but on the other hand he exaggerates in his
mind the element of escapism. The protest, the struggle against op-
pressive external circumstances, is implied, even if the pressures
have not as yet made him bitter. He had emerged not long before
from an education in church schools where there was "a complete
harmony between us and the white teachers at school and between
them and the African staff," as he tells us in his autobiography.[28]
Peter Abrahams, the well-known South African black novelist, who
also attended St. Peter's, says in his book *Return to Goli*[29] that black
Africans on the whole had a more European-oriented education than
white South Africans, since they were largely taught at that time by
clergymen from England or their former pupils. The remoteness of
this background from the South African reality can best be understood when Mphahlele tells us that, at the time, Herrick's lyric on
the briefness of life was his favorite poem.

Recently, when interviewed at the University of Texas and asked
about the stories, Mphahlele said that when he wrote them he had
not as yet felt the political pressures around him. At the time,
however, when the Communist-supported Cape Town weekly,
Guardian, criticized him for forgetting that he is an African and
never letting his characters complain about the pass laws, the pick-
up vans, or the insolence of the white man, he squirmed, he tells us

in the autobiography, because the critic himself was a white man who had never needed to carry a pass, or go through the numerous other humiliations that are the lot of the African.

What hurt Mphahlele more, however, was the refusal of the white press to review his stories as those of a writer but always as those of a black writer. He felt that the reviewers were condescending and patronizing. Only *Trek*, a literary weekly, looked beyond the faulty grammar and stilted constructions to the meaning of the stories. "Instead of blaming fate or God or that popular abstraction, the social system, he — the writer — knows how much of human tragedy is wrought by the ill-will and weakness of people themselves. Thus his stories give us not economic and political theories about human beings but real people giving and taking, hurting and sacrificing; frail noble mortality, unchanging through the centuries beneath all their apparent alteration."[30]

Many white South Africans who read the stories made contact for the first time with an unknown world on their doorstep. There had been three previous works of fiction by black writers with an urban setting: Peter Abrahams *Song of the City*[31] and *Mine Boy*,[32] both published abroad, and *An African Tragedy*[33] by R. R. R. Dhlomo, published by a mission press. White South Africans had been writing about Africans since the last century, but rarely with an urban setting. As in Abrahams' *Mine Boy*, a favorite theme is the country boy come to the city. Mphahlele was the first to portray permanent township dwellers against their own background. Readers had possibly seen "natives" emerge at the suburban railway stations which Zungu in "Man Must Live" calls out: "First stop Mayfair, Langlaagte, Ikona (not) Westbury, New Clare, first stop Mayfair . . ." and heard the shout "U ya phi? Nkosi yam? (where are you going to, My Lord?)"[34] but had never followed the people beyond their destination into their lives.

Mphahlele describes the feeling of seeing himself in print for the first time as "an ecstatic experience."[35] Seven hundred copies of *Man Must Live* were printed by the African Bookman and almost all of them sold. It was to be several years before Mphahlele saw any more of his stories in print.

CHAPTER 2

Beyond Bitterness and Protest

I *Teaching and Dismissal*

S OUTH African journals circulating mainly among white readers
would not accept stories by Mphahlele or any other black writer
unless they had a white background and characters. Mphahlele felt
that he could not prostitute himself to that extent, and there were no
other outlets for his writing until 1953; consequently, he concen-
trated on teaching. The high school in which he taught English and
Afrikaans was the only secondary school in Orlando, and each
classroom held at least sixty pupils. This black township, which today forms part of the greater township of Soweto, was already then
the biggest black metropolis in South Africa, providing inadequate
and mainly squalid accommodation for 100,000 residents.

Right from the beginning Mphahlele loved teaching, and it has
been his first love to the present day. "Teaching is my vocation," he
wrote recently; "on my own terms I do nothing else as successfully."[1] It gave him an opportunity to share his passion for English
literature with others. There has always been an intense rapport
between him and his students. Many of his former pupils in South
Africa and elsewhere still remember him as one of the best English
masters by whom one could ever hope to be tutored. Some have
described him as a man dedicated to his profession and as having a
magnetic personality. One of them recalls the first day Mphahlele
stormed into his first-year matriculation class. He had in his hand a
poetry book, *Eight Poets*, and he immediately started reading
"Kubla Khan" from it. As he recited, he himself became so
enthralled that he almost threw the book out the window.

Four years after joining Orlando High School he obtained the
Bachelor of Arts degree as an external student of the University of
South Africa, majoring in English, Psychology, and Native Ad-

28

ministration. He was now earning £42 a month. Rebecca was also teaching, earning £8 a month. Their first son, Anthony, was born in 1947.

Mphahlele soon made an impact. Although he disliked politics and public speaking, he was drawn into educational politics because of his ability and his fearlessness in expressing his convictions. In November, 1952, he became General Secretary of the Transvaal African Teachers' Association (TATA). In the same year the South African government published the Eiselen Commission's Report, which eventually led to total *apartheid* in education, with an inferior education for the black child. Mphahlele, with others, led the opposition against it in the Transvaal province. In July, 1953, TATA held a conference at Witbank mainly devoted to a discussion on the theme "Education to Change Society." Mphahlele's paper, later printed in the organ of TATA in response to numerous requests, discussed how the new educational code was designed for an educational system adapted for backward communities. The code, he said, after carefully examining its various facets, "does not by any stretch of the imagination meet *our* needs but those of the white man."[2] He urged his colleagues to form their own code. Shortly after the conference, the president of TATA, Mphahlele as its general secretary and the editor of its journal, *The Good Shepherd*, received letters from the Transvaal Education Department dismissing them from the teaching profession in government schools in South Africa. Mphahlele tells us in *Down Second Avenue* what happened subsequently: "A number of pupils decided spontaneously to stay out of school in protest against our dismissal. We were arrested on charge of inciting the boycott and consequently public violence. The three of us were locked up for four days at Number 4 Fort Prison and released on bail. During the trial Crown evidence was given by a number of pupils that they had been taken to the local police station and there forced to sign affidavits to incriminate us, on the threat that they would be sent to the reformatory if they refused. We were acquitted."[3]

There followed a period during which he took various positions. For a short while he taught in Lesotho (then Basutoland) and at his old school, St. Peter's, where Father (now Bishop) Trevor Huddlestone, later well known as a supporter of the urban black man, was then superintendent. By then, the Bantu Education Act, based on the Eiselen Commission Report, had become law. The editor of *The Good Shepherd* described it as unleavened *apartheid* bread, and

Mphahlele saw it as introducing "the threshold of a dark age."[4] St. Peter's, which would not accept the terms of the law, was compelled to close down. Mphahlele's other old school, Adams College, was taken over by the Government and eventually also went out of existence. In 1956 Mphahlele entered his brief and unhappy career as a journalist, when he accepted the position of reporter and literary editor of *Drum*.

II   Drum

The idea of a journal for Africans in English was conceived by Bob Crisp, a well-known white journalist, broadcaster, and sportsman, who envisaged a vehicle for all black African art forms. Since he lacked the necessary funds, he asked Jim Bailey, younger son of a Rand millionaire and racehorse owner, to finance him. This was in 1951, and Bailey is still connected with the publication as it appears today. They were joined after a few numbers by Anthony Sampson, who had been at Oxford with Bailey. Sampson gives the following account of what he found when he took over the editorship:

It was a sixpenny monthly magazine, written in English printed on cheap yellow newsprint; the bright cover showed two Africans facing each other, symbolically, across the continent: one in a Western hat and suit, the other with African skins and assegai.
   The first numbers contained African poems and stories; articles on "music of the Tribes" and "Know Yourselves" recounting the history of the Bantu tribes, installments of *Cry, The Beloved Country;* features about religion, farming, sport and famous men; and strip cartoons about Gulliver and St. Paul.[5]

It did not take Sampson long to discover that a story with a subheading "True Story of How a Brave Man loved an African Chief's Favorite Daughter," with its explanation of native custom, might appeal to European readers, but held no interest whatsoever for the black people of Johannesburg whom he was learning to know. *Drum* was making the mistake of stressing the exotic and the naive, neither of, which meant much to the African in the towns.

Bailey and Sampson thereupon proceeded to give their readers what they now believed they wanted. Crisp left in protest. Gulliver and the Bible were replaced by American comic strips featuring Negro heroes, and all tribal references were eliminated. More African journalists were taken on the staff. One of these was Todd Matshikiza, who was later to gain fame as the composer of the black musical *King Kong.* According to Sampson, it was mainly Mat-shikiza who transformed *Drum.* "He wrote as he spoke, in a brisk tempo with rhythm in every sentence. He attacked the typewriter like a piano."[6] They called his style "Matshikese," and this became the style of *Drum,* often degenerating into comic-book, "tough" prose.

In *Drum* the black man could give expression to what one of its contributors, Peter Clarke, described as a virile, passionate, con-scious entanglement with their lives. They sought, as another con-tributor and staff member, Can Themba, put it, to gain the fullest expression of the bubbling life around them and the restless spirit within them. *Drum* came to represent black literature in English in South Africa for almost a decade. While attempting to compete for African readership with the imported tabloids in providing pin-up pictures and gory reading matter, it also gave a voice to writers who had no other outlet at the time.

Mphahlele's objections to his career in journalism were various, but one he does not mention outright is a well-justified feeling that he was too good for the job. By the time he joined *Drum* he held the degree of B.A. Honors in English literature. As a black reporter, however, even his colleagues, if they were white, thought of him as little more than a slightly literate "boy." He reports the following conversation with the feature editor of the Johannesburg daily eve-ning newspaper, *Star,* who interviewed him as a potential feature writer to represent the "black man's point of view":

"Would you be interested?" the big man asked.
"Depends on the kind of thing you want."
"Have you ever written a regular feature before — for any paper, I mean?"
One has learnt to take South African whites literally, so I replied: "I'm on *Drum* and I write regularly for *Golden City Post* — er — that's our sister paper, by the way — a Sunday paper. It's published by *Drum.*"
"Is *Golden City Post* published in English?"
"Entirely."
"Well, you see what we want need not be in terribly good English. We can always knock it up into shape. I know the Bantu have a peculiar turn of phrase when they write in English. But you shouldn't let it worry you, see what I mean?"

Mphahlele continues:

Of course, I saw what he meant — more than he himself was aware of — these poor wretched whites! He meant he had not the right to call himself a

journalist if he did not know the only Sunday paper in the country published
primarily for non-whites — right in Johannesburg. I thanked him for being
considerate about my "peculiar turn of phrase" and was no more interested
to hear about the kind of article he would want.[7]

In his novel, *The Wanderers*, where Timi, the main character,
joins *Bongo*, a monthly magazine, his editor, Steve Cartwright, says
of him: "Never really liked to be a journalist. Had a superior attitude
towards journalists in general. Felt he was prostituting himself."[8] At
times Steve couldn't bear "his sullen moods, his conceits." The
owner of *Bongo*, Don Peck, asks the editor to tell Timi to produce
some more "luscious scandals" and "exciting political stuff." Steve
replies: " 'You know Timi's attitude to petty political scandal
mongering!' 'Damn him!' " Peck replies, " 'I told him this is a picture magazine and not a political propaganda sheet. Just drum that
into his teacher's head!' "[9]

A deeper reason for Mphahlele's hatred for magazine reporting,
"which took you to the farthest corners of black frustration, struggle,
fortitude,"[10] he also describes in *The Wanderers*. When Timi was
sent out on an assignment he often became intensely involved in it,
beyond the call of duty. It "sucked [him] in."

It was not just a journalistic venture to me. I did not even care if the story on
paper turned out to be as void of life as a chewed piece of string. I just didn't
care. And whenever my mood sagged as a result of a deep involvement with
the people I was meeting while I was on a *Bongo* story, I ceased to care.
Nothing whatever could again rekindle what enthusiasm had initially driven
me to perform a duty. Then the basic need to earn a living became the sole
drive. Because of this, I became angry and impatient with myself. The pet-
tier I appeared to myself, the more I felt pity for myself and the angrier I
became, and so on the cycle went.[11]

Yet his assignments provided the raw material for much of his
later writing. He admits that the experience on *Drum* showed him
things that he would otherwise not have seen, such as going into
other ghettos besides his own and getting into political events and
other situations as a political correspondent. His experiences as a
reporter became the arena on which his creative emotions were
hammered out. He covered most of the important events of the
period: a boycott of the buses against raised fares, the march of
twenty thousand black women to the government buildings in

Pretoria to protest against a measure forcing women to carry passes, and finally his swansong for *Drum*, a trial of 156 men and women for high treason.

His reports are well researched and factual, but with a personal touch that involves the reader and makes him part of the scene. He brings to his report the same sustained feeling of vividness that characterizes his later stories. The report on the bus boycott, for instance, headed "The Boycott that has Become a War," he introduced as follows: "The 50,000 residents of Evaton live in mortal terror. They suspect one another. You meet the people and talk to them. They are very comely and no one looks sick or anemic like the typical townsfolk. They show a fat sense of humour. But somewhere you sense a sickness in the air."[12]

Always he allows the facts to speak for themselves and uses discrimination in picking out points of interest to his readers. For his report on the treason trials he interviewed prisoners and reported what had been happening to them during the nine months they were awaiting trial; how some had married, become parents, studied for degrees.

He surely could not have disliked his task of acting as a literary editor of *Drum*, even if most of the time he felt like "a bull without a China shop."[13] It enabled him to help talented black writers have their stories published — men such as Richard Rive, James Matthews, Peter Clark, or Nimrod Mkele, many of whom have since become well known. In *The Wanderers* Timi felt that *Bongo* magazine would do better to acknowledge the political realities of the country, yet he knew that it provided reading matter in a country where there was little that was elevating and entertaining for the black man to read. Mphahlele did object strongly, however, to the "wet sentimental sexy stories and tough crime stories"[14] which he was supposed to let in. He tried to argue that *Drum*, without becoming snobbish or intellectual, could shape its readers' taste, since they had not as yet developed any of their own, but he was told by Bailey that this was not *Drum's* mission.

The use which Mphahlele made of his experiences as a reporter becomes evident in much of his writing, especially, as we have already seen, in his first novel, *The Wanderers*. Timi gives a realistic account of his exposé of slave labor on a potato farm at "Bethesda." *Drum* had carried such a story about a farm in Bethlehem, written by a reporter whom Mphahlele admired tremendously.

III   *The* Drum *Stories*

Mphahlele's most important contributions to *Drum* were his own
short stories, published between the years 1953 and 1957. He claims
that he developed as a writer in spite of *Drum*, yet, without *Drum*,
he would have had almost no outlet for his fiction before leaving
South Africa. However, he never succumbed to the *Drum* style. The
brash, devil-may-care attitude of the *Drum* journalists was foreign to
him.

When a man knows that he is going to be hurt and insulted at any
time during his waking hours, he must find some means of steeling
himself against the stings. The creative artist, especially, must use
some form of defense, in order to maintain his sensitivity.
Psychologically, though not creatively, it may be best if he gives vent
to his feelings in bitter protest. Alternatively, the writer may hide
behind satire or cynicism, or he may escape into the sphere of
romanticism. Mphahlele, however, has spent his life in taming his
bitterness by facing it squarely and looking beyond it to that "beauty
in man, that thing in man which has permanence and stands the test
of political change."[15] Often he found it impossible. He explains the
difficulties in *The African Image:*

Imagine that you lived in an African or Coloured location.
You had to travel fifteen miles each way between the location and the
town where you worked. . . .
Out of the train, you had to look for the exit meant for *you* as a non-white
person. As you converged with the whites in the city streets again, you ran
into another sharp reminder: police stopping Africans for passes and queues
of people who had fallen foul of the pass law. You got through because by a
stroke of luck you had remembered to take your pass with you. Once work
had started, you didn't know what might happen between you and a white
boss or foreman or the shop assistant or the post office clerk, whose presence
hovered over you like some monstrous explosive thing.
When you reached home the same way you had left in the morning, maybe at 9 p.m., you felt physically tired and spiritually flat. You tried to settle
down to writing. Your whole being quivered with latent anger; words,
words, words spilled on to the pages, and you found yourself caught up in
the artistic difficulty of making a parochial experience available to the bigger world on terms that may very well be possible. For then you had to give
an account of your bitterness. Blinded by it, in addition to other things, you
had to grope for the truth. Somewhere in this dark alley, you felt it was a
hopeless fight because so much of your energy went into the effort to adjust

yourself to the conditions which threaten every moment to crush you. You had to abdicate, as so many others had done and were doing, or write escapist stuff, or get out of your native habitat.[16]

For the moment, however, Mphahlele did none of these things. Instead, he interpreted the effect of the pressures around him on the people he knew best, in terms of fiction. "In them (I wrote a number of things that I still have manuscripts of and which have never been published in book form) I put the ghetto people aside, by themselves, acting out their dramas but at the same time implying the political pressure over them."[17]

Thus we get continuous interplay in these stories between the people and their actions and the background against which they act them out. We have the bitter paradox, for example, in the first of a series of sketches entitled "Lesane," between the joyful news of a wedding and the sordid surroundings through which it is born.[18] In the same story Mphahlele gives us brief pen-portraits of the various guests invited to the wedding and presents a living accusation through the circumstances of his or her life. There is Ma-Ntoi, for instance, "who came from a mining town in the Free State from which she had been expelled because she couldn't own a house as she was a widow"; and Shigumbu, a bachelor from Nyasaland who was trying desperately not to annoy the authorities so as not to be sent back there. These details introduce us to the fullness of township life, with its mass of people from different areas and ethnic groups: a Xhosa and a Basotho, for example, compare their wedding customs. There are rich and poor, educated and ignorant, yet they form a homogeneous whole. This unity is an aspect that Mphahlele later often stresses in his essays. Here he gives it dramatic life. It is this element — "all this," as he refers to it — which gives life a spirit of permanence, despite yesterday's riotous beer-spilling raid and tomorrow's pass and tax raid. The young people, dancing outside in the street, feel it, even if today seems just "a chunk of sweetened and flavored Time."[19] Two old women sense it, as the contrast between "these broken purposes and bigger purpose of living weaving itself somewhere with the passage of years."[20]

Mphahlele describes the daily activities of the township people whose lives are ruled by trains. They board and emerge "savagely"; they are spewn out like "the live vomit of some monster in a folk tale." They pour through the barriers like lava. At the end of the

week you had to "sprawl and stretch your body out so as to feel
something palpable settling down in you, or something ooze out of
you."[21] In this state a man beats his wife and children, a boy digs
his knife into human flesh, and the Zionists sing their half-pagan,
half-Christian songs, Mphahlele tells us, before he goes on to
describe an incident of violence. The ability in penetrating collective
psychology and motivating the actions of a crowd which he shows
here, raises Mphahlele's early works above the protest writing of his
contemporaries. His aim was to reconstruct character "in broader
perspective,"[22] a responsibility, he later felt, that black South
African writers had been shirking in their obsession with race
relations and the facile plots they provided.

Mphahlele has, however, himself been accused of paying more
attention to the development of events in his stories than to people.
Asked about this with reference to *Down Second Avenue* by students
during an interview at the University of Texas at Austin, he was in-
clined to agree, but not altogether, since the people themselves, he
explained, were part of these events.

In these early stories there are only black characters. The white
world outside the township is felt as an elemental force, disembodied
and powerful. In one scene a father reprimands his son for arguing
with the white foreman at his place of work, and thus losing his job.
"Do you know the might of the white man?" the father asks, and
defines this might as that of many arms flapping over you like wings
of a giant bird. The son, Fanyaan, on his first contact with the world
outside, sees white people as a different and incomprehensible
species. "They just looked ahead of them; unfriendly, uncompromising, self-possessed, mysterious, just dumb." A crowd of black
people, on the other hand, is made up of its living human components, whether they are spilling out of a train, gathering for a
violent attack on an Indian hawker, or congregating for a wedding
celebration.

" 'She is there!' When the Africans say a person 'is there,' they
mean you cannot but feel she is alive; she allows you no room to
forget she was born and is alive in flesh and spirit,"[23] Mphahlele tells
us in his autobiography. The people of the ghetto in his stories are
almost all very much "there." They are drawn in the round, with
lives surmised outside the action of the stories, rather than serving
the purpose of the plot or of an idea. In "Reef Train," for instance,
the main character is an eighty-year-old farm worker who has to

make the fearful journey into Johannesburg to see his ailing sister. Although the plot concerns the old man's fear and how it almost became justified, he is not presented as a simple country yokel. He allows himself to be lectured by his wife on how to go through the mechanics of the train journey and merely smiles frequently at her pretence to sophistication. His fear is not that of clean and simple country living for the evils of city life; it does not arise merely out of bewilderment, but out of the deeper understanding of an old man who knows the ways of men. Sitting in the train, with something of the rock-like strength and silence of the land about him, he sees and hears the frantic noise of the city; the workers pouring into the station and into the train, moving as one body to make room for the conductor, a concertina behind him screaming a tune foreign to him, and the wheels of the train carrying on "their own babble-talk like an idiot," while the voices of the passengers float on the crest of the din, shouting with laughter. "Then he remembered the words of his old, old fathers: the great death makes you laugh: sadness in humour and humour in sadness."[24]

Quick sketches of minor characters make an immediate vivid impression, as for instance: "Seleke's cousin came staggering onto the step. . . . He was always referred to as Seleke's cousin and nobody ever cared to know his name.

Seleke lived in the next street. She was the tough sort with a lashing tongue. But even she could not whip her cousin out of his perennial stupor."[25]

All Mphahlele's writing is stamped with a tremendous compassion for humanity. This is the basis of all his thinking, writing, and living. It comes through in his passion for teaching and for literature, and it led him, against his inclination, into politics, public speaking, and finally into exile. To his fiction he brings a deep and warm understanding for the foibles of the weak. A defrocked *moruti* (parson), in the stories about the Lesane family, whose confidence tricks and small airs do little harm, is treated with gentle irony. The *moruti* is a self-employed social worker and self-appointed chaplain to a domestic workers' association, whose members come to his office on their free day and are duly admired and patted on the back. The association ceases to exist and there is talk of misuse of funds, but it evaporates. After that, every morning, the *moruti* goes mysteriously to work, entering the last third-class carriage and walking through to the second, greeting everyone on the way. The *moruti* is human in his weakness but he does not stand as a symbol for this one characteristic. He can pull himself together when necessary and give comfort to a young girl who comes to him in distress. China, in the story "Across Down Stream,"[26] is a man who has killed and is ready to kill again, but he has a tender love relationship with the girl who serves coffee to factory workers. Love is not often the theme in Mphahlele's stories, but this story shows that it is by choice and not through lack of ability to express the nuances of tenderness and conflicting emotions. We see the relationship between these two people from both sides. Pinkie, the coffee-cart girl, both pities and fears China, and China resents her pity and pities her in turn.

In Pinkie we have the first of Mphahlele's typical young girls. Like most of his characters, she has a counterpart in his own life. Rebone, in his autobiography, is his childhood sweetheart, though we must remember that *Down Second Avenue* began as a novel, and there is no proof of what is fiction and what is fact. Pinkie, Rebone, Diketso in the "Lesane" series in *Drum*, and finally — though drawn in finer vein — Karabo in "Mrs. Plum,"[27] are girls of the slums who are moved by an inner strength to try and drag themselves out of their circumstances. Sometimes, tragically, they fail, but they do not despair. His older women we can often imagine as the mature version of the younger girls. Ma-Lesane in *Drum* and Aunt Dora in *Down Second Avenue* no longer have ambitions for themselves, but the toughness and refusal to give in to circumstances is still there. They rule their families with a hand of iron, but with tremendous affection, and thus give their children a sense of mental stability in their unstable world. We know that Mphahlele never moves far from his own experience, and thus feel that in these portraits of the older women he is paying tribute to those who shaped him and enabled him, under impossible conditions, to rise to the position that he holds today.

Although Mphahlele's stories are often less vehement in content than others published in *Drum* at the time, they have a more stirring effect. This is due to the feeling of tangible reality and aliveness which he succeeds in creating. Not only do the people live and move and interact, but the whole setting seems in constant motion. Moroka township, in the earliest of the *Drum* stories, "Blind Alley,"[28] is a monster of no name and no shape, with deadly paws. It screams in pain, sloth, and sordidness. The aftermath of a riot is the shattering cry of the city, which shoots up, hangs in the misty air, and falls into groaning and wailing fragments. In the "Lesane" stories it is Nadia Street, and not just the people living in it, that is so deceptively quiet and, at the end of a riot, resumes its week-day look of innocence.

Most of the stories come to grips with the movement and action of their setting right from the beginning. A favorite technique is to introduce the story with a long, wide-sweeping movement, followed by a short, sharp act or sound. In "Across Down Stream" a crowd of strikers moves like one mighty being and sways and swings like the sea. Then there is a crash as one of a row of coffee carts topples over. In "Down the Quiet Street" the bustling slum activities are described, followed by the crash of a falling coffin.

Intangibles come alive. In the first "Lesane" story a wedding is to take place, and the news spreads rapidly through the township. It first shoots up and down Nadia street like an electric current. But by the time it has gone over the dilapidated houses, percolated through wooden and cardboard paper windows, and the flies, hovering over the dirty water, have buzzed around it, all the joy has gone out of it. It is now being "lashed about from tongue to tongue in the greasy, sticky darkness of Newclare rooms."[29]

Similarly, the old man's fear in "Reef Train" becomes a thing with almost a life of its own. It is described in terms of movement, of a creature that plays an eternal mad song on his nerve strings and strokes his flesh with cold, cold fingers and then, now part of him, throbs in his temples. Day-to-day existence is described in terms of effervescence and movement and noise. "Saturday. The weekend was around again to bottle up the people's weariness, their anxieties, their pains. They would pick up the bottled mixture the next Monday; the mixture picked for them to eat up again before they ran for the train on Monday. And so the cycle went on. And when the black masses poured out of the trains a strange buzzing noise would begin."[30] The noise would rise to a wicked pitch, later the darkness would muffle it.

Most of the stories end on a quiet note, not necessarily of peace, but rather, as in tragedy, of calm after turmoil. In one story there is devastating despair. A couple, Mieta and Saul, always drunk, quarrel viciously and endlessly while their deaf and backward child looks on. They run away, abandoning the child, who is choked to death by the strap that ties him to his bed. "There were urine pools and stools all over the floor. The sooty walls told a murky story of degenerate backyard lives, a rickety cupboard lay on its side and lifesize cockroaches glided merrily in and about as if nothing had happened. The window was shut. There was nothing else, except death."[31]

IV   The Plots: "Blind Alley"

The first of the stories, "Blind Alley," begins with an exposition of the desperate surroundings:

Squalid sack shanties calling. Squalid narrow streets repelling and calling. Some lose themselves here. Others don't. Some lose their hates, loves; others stick out their jaw and live above the flat shanties, the dirty streets swarming with flies. Many revolt against these things, against their wives, their husbands, their parents. But Moroka continues to sprawl up the hill, made by the people in it, making the people in it.[32]

In this story the characters are still sketchily drawn and the plot is naive. We know little about the main character, Ditsi, other than that he is a good man who builds his house and loves his wife; we learn nothing at all about the wife Thamila. Ditsi has to contend not only with John, a "man of the world" who covets his wife, but also with the vicious beast that is Moroka township. Moroka becomes the other woman in Ditsi's life. It takes possession of him and drags him into its political struggles. The theme, as so often in these stories, concerns the potentially tragic ironies of life. Ditsi has helped in a rebellion for better and safer houses, only to find that he no longer has a home to house. His wife has left him for John. Unfortunately, Mphahlele does not stop here, but allows the irony to become pointless melodrama. Thamila returns to him but too late. Ditsi has killed a man in the riots, and in the middle of a sentimental reconciliation scene the police come for him. In this story Mphahlele still lacks the experience of handling plot realistically, and the only character that comes alive is the township of Moroka.

V   "Reef Train"

This story appeared in the *Drum* issue of August, 1954, under the pen name of Bruno Esekie. In the same issue is an installment of Peter Abrahams' autobiography *Tell Freedom*.[33] We can well imagine Mphahlele, on his own daily dreary journey to his job, looking at the people around him, imagining their particular lives, their hopes, and their fears. There, near him, possibly sat an old man, obviously from the country, and showing his apprehension of city ways. Opposite, perhaps, sat a typical youngster of the city slums. What if the old man thought he was about to be attacked? Here was the beginning of a plot, and by the time he arrived home, Mphahlele was possibly ready to write the story.

The old man Moshe was confident in a world where, as a herd-boy, he had been able to get a whole congregation of birds to take off from the cornfield. In this new world, into which he ventures in order to visit a sick sister, there is also a swarm flapping around him, but he has no power over them. He is thus ready to become a victim when three boys come charging through the train, robbing and terrifying the passengers. One thing the old man has left out of his wise speculation about the modern world, and that is the strength of the human heart which can lead to mysterious physical strength. This miscalculation, this failure to recognize humanity when it comes in different guise, lends an ironic twist to the story. Moshe has been terrified of the young boy opposite him. But the boy is his sister's adopted child — "he cannot speak well, but we understand him and he understands us," we learn later — who has made the journey in order to protect his uncle. He does in fact rescue him from the *tsotsis* (hood-lums). Moshe, now understanding fully, laughs heartily at himself. He knows he has been taught a lesson in humanity.

VI "Across Down Stream"

"Across Down Stream" is the story of love between a worker on strike and a girl who sells coffee and pancakes from one of a row of carts outside the factory whose workers are striking. The girl, Pinkie, meets the boy, China, when the crowd of strikers and spectators push over a couple of the carts and China extricates her from the debris. He disappears, but later in the morning, when the crowd has cleared, he comes back to see her. Although this is a tender love story, there is no attempt at escape from reality here — nothing sentimental about Pinkie, dressed in a faded green man's jersey too large for her, a skirt, and a soiled black cap on her head; or China, accustomed to violence, who threatens her with a knife when he feels she is accepting the attentions of an Indian. They never confess their love for each other. "China panicked at the thought of a love affair and remained dumb."[34] We meet them only in the squalid industrial area where Pinkie mans her cart. They are two lonely but proud young people in a cruel world. Although out of work now, China will not accept food for nothing from Pinkie. " 'You'll starve to death in this cruel city,' " she says. " 'And then? Lots of them starve; think of this mighty city, Pinkie. What are we, you and me?

If we starved and got sick and died, who'd miss you and me?' "[35] But they have each other. With his first earnings in a new job he buys her a present.

After his very real threat to kill her in jealous rage, he musters up courage to see her again, but when at last he comes to the usual place, the carts have been abandoned. The law has stepped in, and the carts are no longer allowed to operate. China does not know where to find her. "We'll meet in town, some day," he says to himself as he sits in the empty cart.[36] This vignette of township life set in a sordid frame presents a moment of love and happiness destroyed by human passion and inhuman circumstances, wiped out as though it had never been.

VII   *The Lesane Stories*

The Newclare series of stories about the Lesane family were published over a period of more than a year. Much later, when critics claimed that *The Wanderers* was not a novel, Mphahlele replied that in art your purpose dictated the form. In the Newclare stories we have short pieces of narration, fragments of lives seen sometimes as a silhouette against the background, more often in three dimensions, but always in full motion. This form is the ideal vehicle for what Mphahlele has to tell us.

The first story, "Down the Quiet Street," introduces us to life in Newclare. Nadia Street, considered more quiet than others, has its moments of tension. There is incident rather than plot, yet Mphahlele shows that he has now mastered the technique of short story writing. As usual the background is introduced in dramatic terms and with a statement of events to come: ". . . Things always went on in the *next* street."

"Then something happened. When it did, some of the residents shook their heads dolefully and looked at one another as if they sensed a 100 years' plague round the corner."[37] But we must still wait before anything happens. Cleverly, the characters living in the quiet street are introduced in terms of their reaction to the events still unknown to the reader. A party of mourners now comes down the street carrying a coffin. There is no body in it, though, but a generous supply of illegal liquor. The leader becomes nervous and lifts his side too quickly. It drops, cracks, and bottles spill out.

The editor of *Drum,* in introducing the Newclare stories, described them as a funny, funny piece of comedy. Like the above incident, they *are* often very funny, but of course, as we have seen, all is not rollicking fun. Always the bitter undertones can be heard.

The hero of "Down the Quiet Street" is Tefo, a policeman. He tries to do his duty, but he is stunned by the coffin incident and fails to arrest anyone. The culprits scatter, others pick up the bottles, and one woman asks him for permission to use the box for firewood. Tefo represents the morality of the township, which we meet time and again in black South African fiction. It demands fierce loyalty to one's own, but considers the white man as fair game. Tefo does not follow this principle consciously — he feels that he always conscientiously performs his duty — but his superiors consider him too human to be a good protector of the law. There is no real conflict between law and lawbreaker.

All the Newclare stories deal with the drama of everyday life. Mphahlele's raw material is not the melodrama with which he was also well acquainted: the arrests, the raids, and the brutality. Weddings and funerals, a young man's first acquaintance with the city, poverty, and illness — these are the things that interested him. Both as a result of his wide reading and through an instinctive gift for narrative, he realized that he must write of what he knew intimately. While the editors were still describing the stories as being about "that crazy mixed up family," the Lesanes, the readers must have been aware of the stark, somber reality which always lay waiting in the background of their lives, ready to pounce.

We meet the Lesane family in the December, 1956, issue of *Drum*. The oldest son's wedding is being celebrated in a curious mixture of tribal custom and modern city style. A sentinel at the door of the groom's house, according to custom, demands a goat from the bride's people. "How much is a goat?" asks Seleke, the shebeen queen. "Two pounds and five shillings," is Ma-Sibiya's reply. "It was one pound five shillings before meat control, wasn't it?"[38]

The elders want to make sure that things are done strictly according to custom. One old man feels it is right that the groom and bride move out right away. "If you can rear your own cow, why let others do it?"[39] By contrast the groom's sister, Diketso, is defying convention by having a secret love affair. According to township ethics, parents must be obeyed, though other accepted norms of behavior need not apply. "In town here your honesty can only carry you to the end of Nadia Street,"[40] says one of the wedding guests.

We now hear about the Lesane family in detail and find that their existence is not a "funny, funny piece of comedy" at all. The "bigger purpose of living" is often lost in the desperate day-to-day struggle against poverty: What hope is there for this huge family, housed in two rooms, which Ma-Lesane desperately but unsuccessfully tries to keep clean? The father, discharged from the mines because of ill health, is afraid of his wife and beats his teen-age daughter to prove his masculinity. The younger boys eat their supper secretly in turn, so that they need not feel obliged to invite their friends to share their meager meal. Diketso's lover lives in a squatter's camp among refugees from gang violence. Diketso herself realizes that she is hurting her family and herself by defying her parents and going to her lover, but this is the only way she can combat her frustration at having to leave school early because her parents can no longer afford to keep her there. The episode — if one can call it that, since there is little narration — ends on a slightly more hopeful note. Diketso has not given up all hope and aspirations. There must be a future for her, she feels. And even the present has some happy moments. Unexpectedly, her lover gives her a birthday gift.

The next episode (January, 1957) is about Diketso's eighteen-year-old brother Fanyaan. The autobiographical element is strong here: like Mphahlele, Fanyaan was away in the country for some years with a relative and has now come to join the family in the township. He is behind in his schooling, and is consequently taunted by the teachers and pitied by the children. His mother takes in washing, and Fanyaan carries it to and from the white people's houses after school. Once he is arrested for not carrying his pass. The law is a terrifying, inhuman machine to the boy. Later he is arrested again, for unwittingly fetching *dagga* (marijuana) for Seleke, the shebeen queen. He is freed, however, when Seleke bribes the policeman in charge. She tells Fanyaan's father to teach the boy to be less afraid of the police, since he was caught when he attracted attention to himself by running away at the sight of a patrol. Fanyaan's father feels that it is time the boy went out to work.

The third installment (February, 1957) continues Fanyaan's career, which still runs parallel to that of the young Ezekiel. We follow the timid, likable youngster as he walks down the road, suddenly dodging as he imagines policemen converging on him like birds on a cornfield. His experiences are those of all black men in the city. There is the clerk in the government office who will not give him a permit. "You weren't born here," he sneers at the boy, after firing a series of questions at him. He must name the number of churches in Sophiatown, for instance, and tell how many schools and streets there are. Fanyaan loses his first job because he argues with the white foreman. He is growing up fast, however, rapidly learning about the ways of the city. Disillusioned with his young life, Fanyaan refuses to go to church. Diketso still sees her lover. Old Lesane, the father, feels defeated by the revolt of his children, and he and his wife worry about how Fanyaan will find another job.

The scene shifts to Ma-Lesane at home during daytime, telling Diketso to look out for the vegetable hawker. The action, which has been palling a little, now speeds up, gradually building up a scene of ugly savagery. Mphahlele prepares for the sudden change, from the steady pace of daily trials to an eruption of crowd violence, by a subtle analysis of crowd brutality as the bursting of a bottled mixture of weariness, anxieties, and frustrations.

The incident is introduced with deceptive mildness. The Indian hawker, Moosa, and his little girl appear with their fruit and vegetable cart. A man buys an apple, bites into it, and finds it rotten. He shows it to Moosa, who apologizes and gives him another one. Playfully, the man throws the rotten apple at him. People begin to collect and start throwing fruit around, at first in fun, but gradually more and more vehemently until eventually they upset the wagon and manhandle Moosa. Fanyaan rescues Moosa and his daughter from the crowd. The episode ends when Moosa and the little girl, both in tears, return to the wagon. Nadia Street, at sunset, "seemed to be panting tired after a jolly good laugh."[41]

The sequel is in the next installment (March, 1957). Nadia Street has resumed its look of innocence and Ma-Lesane starts a collection for Moosa. It would have been easy here for Mphahlele to exonerate the crowd, but he avoids the pitfall of sentimentality as well as of cynicism. Ma-Lesane does get a little support, but not enough, and her scheme of paying him back his losses never materializes. One of the children wants to know why the people ran wild and attacked the innocent Indian hawker who had always been their friend. Ma-Lesane's reply uses a simile which explains township life better than any sociological document could do. She says: "This is how, my children: if you put your foot hard on a heap of pebbles, you'll hear them grate and you'll feel them push one another outward. It's like that with us. There's something big on our shoulders, and so we stab and curse and beat one another."[42]

Toward the end of the series there appears to be less and less hope. Diketso is in despair because she hates her work in a factory and sees no way out. She makes a last bid for a better life by confiding in the *moruti*. He promises to speak to her parents. When a neighbor, Ma-

Mafate, misunderstanding the defrocked parson's sympathy for the girl, makes snide remarks about their relationship, Diketso forgets the customary respect toward one's elders and slaps the old woman in the face. The final episode (April, 1957) is the tragic story of a neighboring couple who abandon their child. But, man must live, and so "Nadia street life went on as usual like a printing press."[43]

On the surface the series ends on a pessimistic note. It was certainly written at one of the most mentally devastating periods of Mphahlele's life. Throughout, however, there is a note of hope in the spirit of toughness of the individual people who refuse to buckle under the circumstances and continue to aspire to a better life.

Mphahlele had by now acquired an easy mastery of prose through which he was able to evoke the particular mood he wanted to create. He could switch convincingly from gentle humor to grim realism. The cousin of the shebeen queen in the "Lesane" series is known to the children as "the uncle with the government trousers" because the policemen who come to drink at the shebeen give him articles of clothing from old uniforms. Seleke herself gives a brittle account of her life, which, she says, like that of most people in the township, is a matter of "School, no money, school, no money, out, factory, out, no money, marriage, out, lie, cheat, bribe, live."[44] Just before the horrifying scene after the death of the child is a humorous description of the illness of the child's father. Lesane says it is due to "too much drink going up to a head too full of books and English running around without use."[45]

The dialogue is an effective mixture of contemporary slang and township expressions. "Oh, spirits [of my grandfather], where was this boy when brains were being rationed,"[46] exclaims Lesane in despair over his son. Mphahlele's similes and metaphors are always simple and graphic, usually in direct speech to emphasize a meaning or throw further light on a character, as for instance in Ma-Lesane's comparison of life in the township with a heap of pebbles pushing one another outward.

No further stories by Mphahlele appeared in *Drum,* and eventually he abandoned fiction altogether for many years. How readers of *Drum* reacted to the "Lesane" stories, which they found squeezed between the pin-up photographs and the cartoon features, is not known. The series has never been published in book form. Today Mphahlele feels that they contain something of value and that perhaps he will publish them one day. That would be desirable not only for their intrinsic value but for an account of locale and period which cannot be found elsewhere in such detail. These stories, in addition to *Down Second Avenue,* are as rich a source of information about black city life in South Africa in the 1950's as are the works of Dickens and Gorky about their period. These are two writers whom Mphahlele admired in his early years.

VIII *Academic Successes, Political Involvement, and Departure*

During the period in which he produced the "Lesane" stories, Mphahlele was working for *Drum* and still studying at night. Rebecca was studying for a diploma in social work. She too had left teaching, in protest against the new education act. Ezekiel and Rebecca would wait until the children — Anthony, Terese Kefilwe, born in 1950, and Motswiri, born in 1953 — were in bed so that they could work in the sitting-dining room. In December, 1954, Mphahlele gained the B.A. Honors degree and in December, 1956, he presented his Masters thesis, "The Non-European Character in South African English Fiction," to the University of South Africa. He was awarded the degree with distinction, the first time the English Department of the University of South Africa had awarded a distinction for a senior degree.

Although the University of South Africa, a correspondence university and examining body for external students and university colleges, caters to all students, graduation was racially segregated. The ceremony for black students in which Mphahlele participated took place in a packed school hall in Pretoria in the winter of 1957, and Mphahlele was given a standing ovation. His thesis was later incorporated in his book, *The African Image.*

Mphahlele's activities were not confined to his job, his writing, and his studies, since he would not have been able to exist without imparting his enthusiasm for the arts to those around him. He was active in the Orlando Study Circle, the aims of which were educational and cultural. He particularly enjoyed work with its dramatic group, for which he adapted folk tales and scenes from Dickens for the stage and once put on his own dramatized version of Chekov's "On the Harmfulness of Tobacco." He was also involved in the racially integrated Arts Federation, though he always had reservations about cultural contact with whites. More often than not he boycotted their activities, on the grounds that special appearances by artists for "non-European" audiences, even if they were the only opportunity to reveal top talent, could not be condoned.

In 1955 Mphahlele joined the African National Congress, a

48 EZEKIEL MPHAHLELE

political organization which stood for a nonracial society in South Africa. He was known as a good speaker, with a deep and sonorous voice. The black politicians of the period, the leaders of the Congress and of the rival Pan African Congress, were mainly men who had absorbed politics at the University of Fort Hare. Mphahlele had no natural inclination toward politics and was drawn to it only through force of circumstances: from a sense of personal frustration and through his work at *Drum*.

Among his colleagues on the staff of *Drum* and its sister publication, *Golden City Post* (later *Post*), Mphahlele was regarded as the doyen of the black writers and was always treated with respect. The writers formed a close coterie, meeting regularly at various homes, especially those of Todd Matshikiza and Can Themba. Anthony Sampson concludes an account, "Orlando Revisited," of a party in the black ghetto in which he describes the throbbing jazz music, the elaborate snacks provided, and the mixture of culture and wild abandon as follows: "We slipped away, leaving the shuffling and singing to go on through the night and all through the next Sunday morning, the party guests trapped together by the talk and music like shipwrecked people in a boat."[47]

Mphahlele, however, rarely joined in. He was in the crowd but not entirely of it. He describes his fictitious self, Timi, in *The Wanderers* as "too heavy-footed for the effervescent spirits of the *Bongo* crew, to say nothing of the Sunday *African Sun* lot. I knew they made quips about him in his absence, called him mockingly son of the people, or 'T' for teacher."[48]

At the beginning of 1957 "the little imp in me whispered pesteringly 'Budge! budge!' "[49] He was suddenly seized, he says, with a desire to leave South Africa. Actually the decision was not a sudden one. Repressive laws were mounting and he could not follow the career of his choice. He always knew, like Timi, that "Eventually I would have to decide whether to stay and try to survive; or stay and pit my heroism against the machine and bear the consequences if I remained alive; or stay and shrivel up with bitterness; or face up to my cowardice, reason with it and leave."[50] The reasons were also partly economic: "We were operating our house budget on a miserable income of £40 a month. *Drum* had raised my salary, but it had been pegged at that figure."[51] Another reason was the schooling of his children, who were being taught under a system which, he felt, educated them to be slaves.

Many of his friends tried to dissuade him from leaving. " 'Stay on in the struggle,' they kept saying, 'I'm contributing nothing,' I told them. 'I can't teach and I want to teach, I can't write here and I want to write.' "[52] In September, 1957, he exiled himself, as he put it, in Nigeria.

CHAPTER 3

Down Second Avenue

MPHAHLELE'S autobiography, *Down Second Avenue*, ends with his departure from South Africa. He wrote the first half in South Africa during 1956 and 1957 and completed it in Nigeria soon after he had settled there and begun to teach. In doing so, he was following a trend as well as making a notable contribution: autobiography became a popular form of expression among black South African writers during this time for several reasons. They needed to confirm a sense of identity, particularly those writers who had emerged from the slums and provided their own education. But they wrote the stories of their lives, and found publishers for them, chiefly because direct experience was far more exciting in content and characterization than anything they could invent. The outlets for short stories had practically all fallen away, and none of the writers felt that they had skill and experience sufficient for tackling a true novel. The Afro-American writers whom they admired, James Baldwin, Richard Wright, and others, had all written about themselves.

In an article investigating the psychology of autobiography Bruce Mazlish describes it as "literary genre produced by romanticism, which offers us a picture from a specific present viewpoint of a coherent shaping of an individual past, reached by means of introspection and memory of a special sort, wherein the self is seen as a developing entity, changing at definable stages, and where knowledge of the external world, and both together provide us with a deep grasp of reality."[1] In this sense *Down Second Avenue* is a true autobiography. Just as Mphahlele is spending the years of his exile in a search for racial identity, or an identity of place, as he often calls it, so he was occupied in this work first in establishing a personal identity. Toward the end of the book he speaks of his quest, in describing a visit to Basutoland. "I went to Basutoland in search of something.

What it was I didn't know. But it was there, where it wasn't, inside me. Perhaps it was hate, maybe love, or both; or sordidness; maybe it was beauty. As I say, I didn't know. Once I had landed on the soil of Moshoeshoe's country, the quest seemed never to come to an end. I'm not even sure it has, yet."[2] He goes on to describe his feelings when he stood looking at the sky — "I tried to rip the dark with the razor edge of my desire" — and what he felt when standing on the top of a high mountain: "There I felt the touch of the Ultimate, but only for a fleeting dizzy moment." Then, "for one brief moment of rich promise" he thought. "the secret was in the conical hat and the blanket of a Mosuto standing placidly on the edge of a summit at sunrise." His longing search continued; his mind and heart stood still. It tormented him "to feel so insufficient, and not to know the why and wherefore." Many things became "jumbled symbols" of his hope and yearning: "the purple-pink sunsets; the wasting bleached earth; the rock hanging precariously on the cheek of a hill; the muddy grey waters of the Caledon; the eternal streak of cloud lying stretched out like one of heaven's drunken sots." But alas, he concludes, the dreams "had long since taken flight and now hung dry in shining cobwebs to which my fermenting furies clung crucified. . ."[3]

The purple prose is a shield against exposing his feelings. Mphahlele is, in fact, surprisingly reticent about many aspects of his personal life. The love story of his youth with a girl named Rebone is one of the weakest chapters, for instance, and we never get close to his wife, Rebecca. The search for identity is the theme of the book, but the author as self obtrudes only in occasional deeply personal revelations. This reticence is due to an innate shyness and consequent aloofness, which often led to an inability to communicate verbally with those closest to him and set him apart as a lonely and often unhappy figure. "I felt most bitter," he writes of his mother, "over my inability to thank her substantially for all she had done for me and others. Her abundant love sometimes made me wish we could quarrel."[4]

Yet, paradoxically, he succeeds in imparting the spirit of his experiences. The book was at first envisaged as a novel and is still sometimes regarded as such, in the same way as Camara Laye's *The African Child* and Herman Bosman's personal experiences in a South African prison, *Cold Stone Jug*, are catalogued under fiction. When asked in an interview at the London Transcription. Centre (August, 1969) by Cosmo Pieterse to what extent *Down Second Avenue* was true, Mphahlele replied that perhaps "there is only autobiographical fiction or fictional autobiography in the final analysis."[5] Thus, just as Mphahlele often used autobiographical incidents in his short stories, he inserts sketches in his life story. He used long extracts from *Down Second Avenue* as short stories in magazines and collections, such as "A Winter's Story" in *Fighting Talk*, "The Woman" in *Purple Renoster*, and "The Woman Walks Out" in *Standpunte*.

Whether *Down Second Avenue* is strictly true in fact is of no importance. It is doubtless a true account in spirit of Mphahlele's life and that of the people around him. Even in his avowed fiction Mphahlele never compromises with the truth for the sake of dramatic effect or sentiment, as others are often tempted to do in their autobiographical writing. It seems very unlikely, for instance, that anyone would remember how, at the age of two or three, he tried to lick a raindrop sliding down a windowpane, as does Mphahlele's contemporary and former schoolmate, the black South African writer Peter Abrahams.

I pushed my nose and lips against the pane and tried to lick a raindrop sliding down on the other side. As it slid past my eyes, I saw the many colours in the raindrop. . . . It must be warm in there. Warm and dry. And perhaps the sun would be shining in there. The green must be the trees and the grass; and the brightness, the sun. . . . I was inside the raindrop, away from the misery of the cold, inside my raindrop world.[6]

The incident makes a most effective introduction to the book, but right from the beginning one loses the sense of experience relived, whether tranquilly or still charged with emotions, that Mphahlele succeeds in conveying to the reader. Peter Abraham's *Tell Freedom* is well organized and skillfully executed, the work of a storyteller. Only incidents likely to be of interest to the reader are selected, yet it lacks the impact of Mphahlele's often rambling story. While Abrahams opens his autobiography with a symbolic reminiscence of warmth and security inside a raindrop, Mphahlele, with no artifice, begins his story by admitting ignorance about parts of his early life. "I have never known why we — my brother, sister and I — were taken to the country when I was five."[7]

Abrahams' account of an incident in which a white boss forces the uncle of little Peter to beat the child for retaliating against an attack by white children is strong stuff, designed to make even the hardy reader weep in rage. The only *raison d'etre*, on the other hand, of an incident with as great a dramatic impact in *Down Second Avenue* is that it happened: Mphahlele's drunken father attacks his mother and pours a pot of boiling stew over her head. It is told with an economy of words and no attempt to embellish the drama. Each of the two writers has the same aim, to tell the reader how it feels to be black in South Africa, and how he wrestles with his bitterness and meets the challenge. Peter Abrahams never forgets his audience, whereas Mphahlele continues to look at the world around him and bring it into focus. Here, however, he is more personally involved than he was in his short fiction. He describes himself as sitting on the veranda of a shop in Marabastad. "If you were alone, you were in a position to view critically what you considered to be the whole world passing down Barber Street, half-detached, half-committed."[8]

What, then, is *Down Second Avenue*? We have examined its theme and its purpose. In contents it is a mixture of dramatic action, of sketches, of introspection and comments. It is typical of Mphahlele's writing other than his short stories, in that he refuses to adhere to an established category; yet there is a considerable amount of unity. The story takes us from his earliest memories as a boy of five in the country to his departure from South Africa. The greater part of the book, as the title indicates, deals with life in a street of the black location where he spent his teen years. We watch his world deteriorate politically and socially, and his own tension mount. We follow him to school and college, watch him gain honor and distinction in education, followed by defeat, disillusionment, and finally self-imposed exile. A detailed account of the contents would merely be a repetition of the story of his life, up to the time of writing his autobiography.

It is the control and dramatization of his feelings, rather than the chronology of his life or the scheme to which the contents are loosely organized, that hold the book together. This he achieves without conscious effort. Action often becomes the vehicle of thought or emotional growth. Dramatization of bitter experiences helps him to keep the feeling of bitterness under control. He tells in dramatic terms, for instance, how at the age of thirteen he kept watch while the women brewed beer illegally, and how he was caught and beaten by the police. Then, again, emotion is expressed as a concrete thing that can be felt and tasted. His friend Rebone has taken him to watch a horse parade held annually in celebration of the defeat of the black chief Dingaan of the Zulus. The children are manhandled by the white crowd and thrust out of it. "Tears were gathering in my eyes, and a lump of bitterness stopped in my throat, and I couldn't speak any more. But deep down in the cool depths of this well of bitterness, I felt a strong current of admiration for Rebone. And the cool freshness of it made itself felt deep down in the pit of my stomach."[9]

He is less successful when he cannot feel an incident as real, or identify with a situation emotionally. The tragic story of Dinku Dikae, who is terrified of policemen until the insults of one of them drives him to murder, seems beyond Mphahlele's powers. What should have been tragic climax to the love story of young Ezekiel and Dinku Dikae's daughter, Rebone, is recounted in retrospect and reads like a day-old newspaper story.

Most of the chapters start with a brief general description, followed by an incident which shows how his life is affected by the events or circumstances described. An example is the chapter on beer brewing. It is Saturday night in Marabastad location. The township is steeped in the misty light of early street lamps. There are screams and whistles and curses to be heard. His aunt is making beer as usual while she talks about the necessity of working for the white man. The tins of beer are just being buried. Suddenly, there are heavy footsteps. "Two big men had jumped into the yard, and a big torchlight flashed all over, swallowing up every little object around. Before they turned the corner I had received the tin. In a split second I flung the tin into the next yard. It landed with a splashing thud."[10] Then comes the beating when he refuses to tell the police what he is doing there.

In another chapter Mphahlele describes the church day-school he attends and his grandmother's admiration for the headmaster, which comes to an abrupt end when the man canes Eseki for not attending choir practice. The choir was practicing for the visit of Prince George, Duke of Kent, to South Africa. Eseki could not attend because he was delivering washing that day. The general account is followed by the amusing drama when Eseki's intimidating Aunt Dora confronts the headmaster.

The chapter headed "Ma Bottles" describes Marabastad in winter, the pall of smoke from fire-braziers emphasizing the drabness of the tin houses in the morning light; the open fires in the street with old men squatting before them and children pushing and jostling one another to draw nearer; the women from the country who had come in ox wagons and outspanned on open ground at the end of the location, where they sold sweet potatoes cooked on the spot. Again there is a police raid and the women are told to pack and go at once. As they move there is a wail.

"Jo, Jo-weh!" Then I saw the women dash towards our house, which was the nearest. I carried the dish containing her things after her.

I found grandmother and Aunt Dora bending over her. Grandmother took the child from her, and I noticed that he was limp. The mother seemed off her head.

"He's not dead, no, not my son," she wailed, her hands over her face. "He must be well and strong again. And when he's big he will go to school and learn how to write his name and letter to me. But how can I read his letters? I must work very hard and add another ten shillings to that money to buy him a jersey. Then there'll be two. My man is out of work, he's so head-strong he quarrelled with the white man at work, and he should know you don't go far quarrelling with the white man because he is so strong and so rich. My son mustn't die. *Jo, Jo-weh! Me-weh"*

Aunt Dora was trying to console her.

The child was dead.[11]

Some of the incidents are written almost in the form of short stories, such as the chapter headed "Ma-Lebona" which became the short story "The Woman."[12] It is the tale of the formidable Ma-Lebona, a school teacher in her youth, married three times, who "went into the business of running daughters-in-law," the wives or prospective wives of her weak-willed son. The first wife ends her career by slapping her mother-in-law, and the next bride-to-be fails to show up for the wedding.

More briefly, one of the "interlude" chapters continues the story of Ma-Lebona and tells of her disillusionment even in death. She dies while on a visit to a distant village and is buried in a graveyard with thorn trees and no tombstones, instead of the beautiful graveyard of her choice, clothed in a shroud she had made herself. This incident later became the short story "The Woman Walks Out."[13] The first chapters, about his childhood in the country, give Mphahlele an opportunity to recount tales told around the communal fire-place, like the story of the Christian boy who fell in love with a girl from the pagan community over the river. He and the girl run away from her angry brothers, but the girl is drowned as they cross the river.

Some of the stories or incidents are in a humorous vein. Most end tragically like the story of the sweet potato seller. Life is harsh, and it is here, on Second Avenue, that Mphahlele learns that man must live and make the best of his circumstances. To Ezekiel, even as a boy, living meant mental survival. We see him doing his homework, learning off by heart a "memory lesson," the story of Moses in the bulrushes. Ezekiel is lying flat on his stomach on the bank of a river just below the police station:

There are leafy poplars behind me. The leaves quiver in the lazy midday breeze, causing an interplay of silver and grey and grey [sic]. It is good to know and feel close to the earth, its coolness, its kindness; to feel the blue gum trees pour their shade over you.

I'm not afraid here by the stream. Mr. Goldsmith, the white man whose washing we do, is not here. Not even Mrs. Reynecke — môre kom, or Mrs. Singer — Chobolo. Or even the tottering, withered bones of Miss Forster — Ma-Bottles. The "Market Master" with his huge paw is far away, I don't know where. I shan't see Big Eyes and Kuzwi till Monday.

He begins to dream.

Moses in ark of bulrushes, floating on water. What a beautiful thing to happen to a person to be hidden in a basket. To be so free, so lovable. . . .[14]

What would happen if he found such a baby among the poplars? Why was his mother not born a king's daughter? It must have been these dreams, this search for inspiration in his own mind, that helped him at the time to survive, for there was nothing else for him in Marabastad or in the white people's suburbs to set him on his path as a future writer.

The above is the second of the Interludes between chapters, in which Mphahlele stops the narrative to think. Asked in an interview at the University of Texas at Austin whether these interludes were inserted later, he said that they were written at the same time. He would write about the people and the events in which they were caught up and then literally come to a stop and try to think about what these things were doing to him. He found he could not express this in the strict order of biography, so he decided on the method of the interlude.

In the first Interlude Ezekiel is lying sleepless on the floor of the bedroom, together with his brother and three uncles. On the other side of the room, also on the floor, is his sister. The grandmother and three cousins lie on a double bed. It is almost daybreak and he is still "thinking and feeling," as he listens to the night noises, thinking about school where he still feels "weak, inferior, ignorant, self-conscious," about his fear of the police, about the white man — " 'The white man is strong,' funny this comes to me as I seem to hear my mother say it: the white man's strong I don't know you mustn't stand in his way or he'll hurt you, maybe when you're big I don't know you will open your mouth and say what is in your heart but remember now the white man has a strong arm."[15]

The third Interlude mourns the passing of Marabastad. This Mphahlele does from than one aspect. He deplores the political expediency that led to its disappearance — "They call it slum clearance instead of conscious-clearance" — but he also sees it as symbolic of the black man's being always on the move, of his poverty and despair. It is not the passing of the township he regrets but its existence in the past, in the present, and in the future "until the screw of the vise breaks." On the personal level he mourns, without nostalgia, the people who vanished from his life, dying like Siki, the guitarist, "with his fingers entangled in the broken strings of his instrument." And finally it is a deeply felt mental experience. Marabastad may be gone, but there are many more Marabastads still in existence. It is he who has jumped out of the nightmare and is no longer moving up and down Second Avenue.

As a tribute to a passing township it is perhaps not as effective a piece of writing as Can Themba's often-quoted "Requiem for Sophiatown." With sardonic humor, Themba sums up what Mphahlele takes many pages to say; that the black man in South Africa dare not aspire to Western culture. Themba is speaking of various people who have vanished: "Dwarf, who used to find a joke in everything. He used to walk into Bloke's place, catch us red-handed playing the music of Mozart."[16] Both Themba and Bloke Modisane[17] treat the passing of a slum more realistically than Mphahlele. They wander through the ruins and the loss hits them drastically, "with the sudden crash of a flying brick on the back of your head,"[18] in the case of Themba. Mphahlele is too bitter to indulge in nostalgia for a festering slum. While Themba characteristically mourns the escape-hatches which made life bearable — the shebeens where he mixed his drink with friendship, gossip, and intellectual pursuit — Mphahlele soberly, if guiltily, rejoices that he has found his way out of the nightmare. All of these writers, however, see the dissolution of a community as a symbol of the black man's despair.

Once Mphahlele leaves Second Avenue, the work becomes more conventionally autobiographical. The interest for the reader now lies in his admiration for the achievements of the writer and for his political stand. There is no longer the spontaneity and aliveness of the earlier chapters. The narrative tends to ramble, and the ramifications of the political and the educational controversies are not sufficiently explained to make them clear from a distance in time and place. On the other hand, an imaginary discussion between the two black parties, the African National Congress and the Pan-African Congress, oversimplifies the issues.

There are flashes of malicious fun when he speaks of his dramatic activities. On one occasion a program of scenes from Shakespeare and performances of classical music are taken to a location outside Johannesburg. In the audience is a white mine compound manager who condescendingly discusses the program with the performers before the concert begins. He uses Fanakalo, a pidgin mixture of English, Afrikaans, and several African languages. Khabi Mngoma, one of the artists, answers in the same language. When, at the end of the performance, the mine manager, having seen the standard of production, congratulates the performers in English, Khabi Mngoma replies: " 'Tina zamile, . . . Sibongile stellek, yena moshle stellek lo Scarlatti.' — Well, we've tried. Thank you very much. Scarlatti's very good.''[19]

The book regains its emotional impetus toward the end when Mphahlele describes the most bitter period of his life, culminating in voluntary exile. This he expresses in the Interlude in the mountains of Basutoland, and in the final Interlude in which he wrestles to unlock the cage that imprisons his strivings and desires. To stay and deny inspiration, ambition, and ideals would be the easy way out. Since he wanted to give to life something that was denied to him in his own country, he must leave.

I *It Was Like This on Second Avenue*

In the potpourri of theme and subject matter that is *Down Second Avenue*, one expects, and indeed finds, a variety of styles. When reliving periods of mental and spiritual conflicts and depression, the story seems to stagger and continue in small leaps. As bitterness becomes deeper and his despondency thickens, the writing becomes slower and laden, sometimes overladen, with imagery, as in the extracts from the Basutoland Interlude quoted above. Yet there is always control. Bitterness and anger are never allowed to get out of hand. After the police beat thirteen-year-old Ezekiel in order to obtain information from him about illegal beer-brewing, the chapter ends, not with a homily about the sadistic police, but with an amusing discussion between grandmother and her cronies about the quality of the beer. Some tins, Dokie, the sharp one, swears, have tufts of animal hair in them. "The things witches can do when they want luck in their beer business!" she says. Mphahlele continues: "Most people feared she was telling the truth. Women brewed some of the most terrifying compounds. 'It's heathen!' grandmother said indignantly. 'My beer's the pure and healthy food a man's stomach needs!' "[20]

Whenever the work threatens to become too ponderous there is comic relief. In an early chapter, "Backward Child," Mphahlele has just come to the city. Hungry, weary, feeling inferior at school and afraid of the teachers, he finds relief in attending the movies and meeting his friends there. Soon his English improves and he earns pocket money by reading the captions to the illiterate. He is very much afraid that talking films will put him out of business. Later, at a time when he felt his life was "one huge broken purpose," he worked for an institute for the blind. "I had to look after a batch of blind men in a house in the slummy and rusty location. . . . The blind men came to call the house 'Silver House' because the corrugated iron walls and roof had new silver paint on. They continued to call it so even when, later, I told them it had been repainted green. 'If it bothers your eyes, it doesn't bother ours,' Meshack said simply."[21]

As always, Mphahlele is at his best when describing the active world around him. Second Avenue is presented as it was almost without comment. The graphic pictures portray bitterness as something we can almost grasp in our hands. He is cycling one morning, for instance, from a white suburb with a large bundle of washing on the handle bars. "It was such a cold mid-winter morning that I was shivering all over. I had on a very light frayed and torn blazer. Nose, lips, ears, toes and fingers felt like some fat objects detached from the rest of the body, but so much part of me that the cold burnt into my nerve ends."[22] At a circle he fails to make a right turn because of the pressure of the bundle. From the opposite direction a handful of white boys come cycling toward him. "They took their bend, but it was just when my bicycle was heading for the sidewalk of the bend. They were riding abreast. For some reason or other I didn't apply my brakes. Perhaps my mind was preoccupied with the very easy yet not so very easy task of turning the handle bars. I ran into the first boy in the row, who fell on to the next, and their row was disorganized." The boys kick and curse him as he comes down, then they ride away leaving him "with the cold, the pain, the numbness, and a puncture and bent front wheel." He continues: "I picked up the bundle and dragged myself on to the sidewalk and leant against a tree. At first I was too bewildered to think. I started off again and limped six miles home. My aunt and grandmother groused and groused before they had Oompie's vehicle fixed."[23]

Conditions on Second Avenue are described without asides. This is how it was on Second Avenue. Yes, he says, it had to be thus, always. There is nothing soft and sentimental about the countryside of his early childhood with its dark solid mountains and its people aware of "only one purpose of living, to be,"[24] any more than there is about Marabastad, which he remembers only in the cold and dreary winter, where "time ran out with the same slow relentless and painful flow of tap water."[25]

II *Characters*

Down Second Avenue is by no means a static canvas painted in drab and monotonous tones of despair. It is the aliveness of the characters, and their efforts to rise above their circumstances, that distinguishes this work and sets it above the autobiographies of his contemporaries among black South African writers. Once again the individuals, major and minor, are, like Ma-Lebona, "there" and allow "you no room to forget [they were] born and [are] alive in flesh and spirit."[26]

We learn to know them through incidents in which they are involved or through their casual encounters with each other. Dialogue is always earthy and colloquial, and interspersed with proverbs and literal translations from the vernacular. This often has the effect of providing a touch of humor and further relieving the gravity of the account. The people say of Ma-Lebona and her first husband, for instance, that "the bell rang for stopping work"; in other, far less telling words, he left her.

Mphahlele excels particularly in bringing a group of people to life. In one incident a number of women are standing and chatting at the communal water tap:

"You've never heard of such a thing," said Ma-Janeware, the jet-black woman whose house was the nearest to the tap. "A tortoise in Ma-Legodi's yard, lying restfully against the wall as if it was laying an egg of mischief."
"Who saw it?" asked Dokie the sharp one. She was "the sharp one " because there was another — Dokie the fat one.
"I'm not going to mention names," said the Black woman.
"It's not true then," Dokie the sharp one said.

"Look, it's not my business to be nosing into other people's dark ways, but — don't tell anyone about this. I got it from a goat by the roadside, and you did too if someone asks you. But really Dora whispered it in my ear."[27]

It is an important piece of news that they are discussing, since the tortoises are a sign of witchcraft.

The water tap is a favorite center for events and discussions in black South African fiction, comparable to the village well in Western literature. For Peter Abrahams in *Tell Freedom* it becomes the backdrop for an amusing incident, at the same time demonstrating the hard lot of a child in a location. For Bloke Modisane in *Blame Me on History* it is part of the narrative of his boyhood in Sophiatown and his relationship with his father. Only in *Down Second Avenue* does the scene come dramatically alive for its own sake.

Down Second Avenue, more than the short stories, contains characters one is unlikely to forget. Leading these are Grandmother and Aunt Dora. Mphahlele did not need to embellish his account of these two women. Like life in Second Avenue, this is how they were. Some years later, during a television interview in a Paris cafe in 1964, Mphahlele said that these were the people who impressed him most in life, especially "with the complete control that they had of their lives." Dora was "personally at grips with reality." Grandmother, too, was a realist but "she had this tremendous religious devotion . . . which never forsook her."[28] Grandmother, in *Down Second Avenue,* has a fetching way of talking about the Christian God and the gods of the ancestors in the same breath, without creating any sense of conflict. Dora creates an impression of physical strength, a woman who knew what she wanted and how to get it — now. Aunt Dora is always described in terms of action. She is "Quick to use a clap on one's cheek"; she could "literally fling a man out who took long before paying a debt for beer."[29] Even Ezekiel's schoolteacher was intimidated by her. Grandmother is never described in so many words. She emerges in the course of the narrative, in dialogue and casual comments. She calls Saul and Rieta, for example, a couple who drink too much and are always quarrelling, "Sodom and Gomorrah." When she dislikes someone she makes no bones about saying so. She would question the children's playmates closely about their parents, and if she did not like what she heard she would tell them to stay away in no uncertain terms. One morning, Mphahlele tells us, she had a quarrel with the "woman next door," as she always called her. " 'Sies,' Grandmother hissed, and spat at intervals to show her utter contempt. 'What was your mother, after all? She never knew a pin and she used a mimosa thorn to button up her blouse with and she was a heathen and she was not paid a bride price for and you'll remain poor as you are and eat dogs' meat and rats' meat!' "[30]

The contributary figures of *Second Avenue* are also drawn in the round. Ma-Lebona is the one who is "there." We see her before us immediately, a figure of fun who arouses the scorn of the realists around her. "I remember Ma-Lebona, about fifty, thin, spectre-like; her chest curving in a little; her whole physical make-up seeming to consist of taut strings which would one day snap and bring chaos and hell fire upon the whole township."[31] In her youth she played tennis and when she "talked tennis" now, she often spoke in English to the total dislike and contempt of many of the older folk.

As the main character in a novel, if we are to regard the book as such, Ezekiel emerges without conscious effort. It is unlikely that Mphahlele even realized that he was drawing the portrait of a hero, a man brave and uncompromising when the situation demanded it, yet sensitive, a little aloof, a writer who in another time and place might have turned to nature for inspiration. We watch his emotional growth and his reaction to the forces that mold him. It may seem strange to examine the subject of an autobiography with critical objectivity. Yet it will emerge later, when we look at his second autobiographical novel, *The Wanderers*, that Mphahlele approaches the main figure of this work somewhat differently.

The only poorly depicted character in *Second Avenue* is Ezekiel's childhood sweetheart, Rebone. We meet her first, full of promise, as a newcomer to Marabastad, who proudly walks past the gang of boys without asking the expected questions about school, and who drags Ezekiel nonchalantly into the white crowd on Dingaan's Day. But she does not grow, and her degeneration from model scholar who vied with Ezekiel for first place, into an habitué of dance halls and moll of gang leaders, is not well motivated. As a real-life model, Rebone gains stature in later fiction as Karabo in "Mrs. Plum," and was already more credible as Diketso in the "Lesane" series. Her father, Dinku Dikae, pinpoints the terror with which the average black man views the white world that rules his life. Mphahlele's mother, Eva, is lightly sketched. Mphahlele imparts to the reader his shyness of the woman to whom he knew he owed so much materially, but could not find the words to thank. Rebecca, Mphahlele's wife, and the children, are a part of his life into which the reader may enter only in very brief glimpses.

Except as a force of terror, the white world intrudes little into Marabastad. To the older people the government is a strange person who does strange things. Ezekiel first meets white people when he fetches their washing. He knows only their curses at being disturbed, their averted faces, their excuses for late payment, the fuss they make over their pets. Then Mphahlele leaves the shelter of his environment and of church schools and meets the whites in their business surroundings. They are still unreal for him. He describes his first boss, a lawyer for whom he carried messages: "The proprietor was a tall forbidding colossus. A man I never again uttered a "Good Morning" to after trying a few times without success. Maybe it was because his ears were high above me: he never seemed to hear me. Something about him made me think of Scrooge. I trembled all the time I cleaned his ink pots and the large glass on his table. Our eyes never met, so I came to regard him as a machine that generates power but only from somewhere on the fringe of one's awareness."[32]

Small wonder then that Mphahlele rarely succeeded in portraying a white South African character successfully. He knew them only as non-people. He saw them as types because that is how they deliberately presented themselves to him. The whole system of South African relationships is aimed at making whiteness, not individual features, the important factor. Whether Miss Preston and Miss Chimes in the offices that he visited had characteristics different from those of white girls in other offices was irrelevant to his life. They represented to Mphahlele something negative, a denial of everything that living meant to him. They were simply not "there."

They seemed to do little more than let their bodies sway at their compressed dehydrated hips; perch like brittle china on their seats and paint their nails; pick up a mirror and adjust hair that didn't want adjusting and powder their bloodless faces; hold interminable conversations over the telephone and giggle in a sickening high tone that gave me the itch to hold their jaws opens to get full-throated laughter out of them.

"Wait John," one with a dehydrated bosom would say, "the boss is still busy in his office." While I waited I speculated upon the daily run of these people's lives. While we shouted and laughed in our packed and stuffy trains, in our long weary bus queues, in the buses, they boarded their clean buses and separate train coaches from their separate suburbs — clean, quiet but either dead or neurotic. And at our end of life Black humanity, though plunged into a separate, overcrowded, violent and dark existence; still vibrant, robust, with no self-imposed repressions."[33]

Later in his life, and already during his stay at St. Peter's as a pupil, Mphahlele saw whites as individuals and many became his friends.

There are still flaws in the language of the autobiography; awkward sentence constructions occur and words are occasionally misused. Overdone rhetoric sometimes intrudes, but the narrative flows and, above all, the realistic characterizations are more than enough to compensate. The main thrust of life is "there."

III *Acclaim*

Critics and public alike approved of *Down Second Avenue*. The critics who specialize in African literature, however, often attempted to use the work to illustrate preconceived ideas. Janheinz Jahn, in *Muntu*, saw *Down Second Avenue* as an example of African culture which must always express something and never someone. He claimed that Mphahlele treated his own life "as a symbol of the situation in South Africa" where "every experience becomes a paradigm, every personal oppression a general experience."[34] This may be the result of the way the autobiography was written and a cause for its success, but it was certainly not its author's aim. Wilfred Cartey, on the other hand, called Mphahlele a reactor rather than an interpreter. This view, too, seems to see something other than the author's intention in tackling the story of his life and its meaning. *Down Second Avenue* is meant neither as a symbol of anything nor is it an account of events passing over a passive victim of circumstances. Anne Tibble in *African/English Literature*, which she dedicated to Mphahlele "with respect," summed up one aspect of the work very clearly: "Mphahlele's method with English in his story is to mix a stark and candid realism that now and then drops deliberately into the squalid or the startlingly banal with passages of idealism and involuntary beauty. This exquisite perception of the two poles of life is Mr. Mphahlele's contribution to African prose."[35]

It is interesting to speculate what readership Mphahlele had in mind when he wrote *Down Second Avenue*. He does not appear to be addressing any particular category, unlike Peter Abrahams, who, when his reminiscences appeared, already had a following of white readers abroad, among whom he lived. Mphahlele does not throw in his lot with his fellow black writers, his colleagues on *Drum*, with whom he found it difficult to identify; nor does he attempt to explain the black man to his white fellow South Africans or to the white man abroad. With the black man in Africa and America he had not as yet made much contact. *Down Second Avenue*, then, simply tells the story and those who want to listen may do so. Thousands did. The book was translated into German, Hungarian, Czech, Serb-Croat, Bulgarian, French, Swedish, Japanese, and several African languages. Extracts appeared in anthologies edited by Per Wästberg (*Afrika Berettar*, 1965), Richard Rive, (*Modern African Prose*, 1964), Leonard Sainville (*Anthologie de Literature Negro-Africaine*, 1963), Jacob Drachler (*African* Heritage, 1964), Paul Edwards (*Through African Eyes* and *Modern African Narrative*, both 1966). Doubleday in New York, published an American edition with a new introduction in 1971.

Down Second Avenue is still as relevant today as it was in 1959. As a social record it is unique. As a human document it is more moving than anything that has come out of South Africa besides Alan Paton's *Cry, the Beloved Country* and Olive Schreiner's *Story of an African Farm*.

CHAPTER 4

The Living and Dead

I *Living with Freedom*

SHORTLY after his arrival in Nigeria Mphahlele wrote:

The moment I stepped off at Kano airport in Northern Nigeria. I felt a wonderful sense of release. Being here in Lagos feels like having jumped suddenly out of a nightmare. How else can it be? There I was, on the night of September 6, walking across from the giant KLM plane to the airport offices, to find immigration, customs and other departments all staffed by Africans. And then to be accorded such civility as I could never dream of in any government office in South Africa.[1]

Freedom was a heady feeling, "an exquisite sense of release."[2] He was struck by the self-assurance of the people, by "the lust for life that is not," he said, "as it is among my people in the South, brought into relief because someone is trying to beat it down, because it seeks to vindicate itself." He exulted in moving about where he liked at any time of day or night, without fear of being stopped by a policeman. He found that "the gestures of the people strike a familiar chord as they speak, because you too are African." He felt that, though he was a foreigner, it was not like being a foreigner in one's native land, as he had been at home. He breathed the air of freedom deeply, and "tested its salty freshness" as he stood on a bridge looking out across the glistening ripples of the lagoon.

This was at the beginning. When the first headiness wore off, he found himself only half listening when people spoke to him. "Because you are trying to find your mental bearings." This he has been trying to do ever since, both as a man and as a writer. Then came the sheer personal homesickness, which Timi, chief character in *The Wanderers*, is described as having felt, "of getting to know himself, to know alienation, aloneness, nostalgia, the longing to be back in the fire, just so long as he would be suffering along with others of his kind. He longed for his next-of-kin, for his friends. . . ."[3] Like Timi, Mphahlele missed the sense of community living and also found it of little use, after all, to assume "an immediate common heritage" among Negroes everywhere. "No use," Timi said. "You're an expatriate. Take your chances, tread softly, human cultures have stone walls."[4]

Nor did he always find it easy to live with freedom. It seemed to intensify his hatred of those who had denied it to him. In 1961 the South African government gazette named him as a banned person under the Amendment to the Suppression of Communism Act. His writing could no longer be quoted or disseminated in South Africa. After three years in Nigeria he came to the conclusion that once an exile, always one. A three weeks' visit to London left him "a bundle of agitation."[5] In France he found no commitment and no desire to identify with French intellectual life. What he missed everywhere was an emotional and intellectual commitment to a place. From now on Mphahlele's writing was split in two. He wrote, and still writes, either as a South African in retrospect, or as an African from or about a continent in which he has yet to find his bearings. His wanderings, physical and spiritual, had begun.

The facts of his life are no longer of the same importance to his writing as they were in South Africa. When he writes fiction, the background is often still South Africa, and it does not matter whether he writes in Lagos, Nairobi, Lusaka, Paris or Denver. Although he did not find it easy at the beginning to project his mind into the situation he had left behind, he soon entered a period where the memory sharpened and came into focus again. It reached back to the point, he explains in an interview in Paris,[6] where anger was deep and the hurt sharp and fresh. Writing of South African poets in exile — Dennis Brutus, Mazisi Kunene, Dollar Brand, and Breyten Breytenbach, Mphahlele says:

At the time of severing oneself from South Africa, there appears a mood of placelessness in one's poetry. The concrete stuff thins out; feeling becomes formalized, ideas become dominant. When concrete objects come back into one's verse, they evoke a nostalgia. The imagination dislodges them from their native setting and gives them another place, a nowhere place. It is possible that in permanent exile one can develop a sense of place where one lives.[7]

This was obviously also his experience in his fiction. He soon stopped writing short stories, and his first novels suffer, as we shall see, from his mental placelessness. It is for a sense of place that he is still searching.

Physically, he covered thousands of miles between 1957 and 1970. He arrived in Ibadan in September, 1957, and obtained a post at the University there. In the summer of 1959 he had four and a half months' leave of absence which he spent mainly in Britain. His family had gone temporarily back to South Africa where his son, Chabi Robert, was born in Orlando in July. Another child, Puso, was born in Nigeria in May, 1961.

Mphahlele left Nigeria after three years because of dissatisfaction with his life as a teacher there. He felt that he was being treated as an outsider. In spite of professed Africanization of jobs, it was still easier for a white man than for a black South African to obtain a teaching post. When his appointment was not renewed, and Africanization was given as a reason, the white lecturers on the staff remained. Disillusioned, he went to Paris in 1961 to head the African Department of the Congress for Cultural Freedom, a body founded in the early 1950's to defend intellectual freedom wherever it was violated. Congress business frequently took him to Africa where, on behalf of the Congress, he helped to found the Mbari Writers' and Artists' Club of Ibadan in June, 1961, together with leading Nigerian writers Wole Soyinka and John Pepper Clarke, Frances Admola, a Ghanaian broadcaster, and Ulli Beier, an authority on Yoruba culture. The name Mbari was derived from Igbo religious practice, according to which a Mbari house is built in dedication to the earth goddess. It is always a communal effort and is decorated with wall paintings and filled with mud figures. It is then left to decay and a new house is built, as a symbol that religion needs constant renewal. Mbari thus means a kind of re-creation. The club held art exhibitions, concerts, open-air dramatic performances, and writers' workshops, and it housed an African reference library. A publishing house, Mbari Publications, was founded to publish African writing. Conferences on African culture and writing were held regularly.

This was the kind of activity that Mphahlele supported with enthusiasm. In 1963 he went to Nairobi for three years. He set up the Chem-chemi Cultural Centre, again on behalf of the Congress for Cultural Freedom, although actually founded by the American Fairfield Foundation. By then there were three Mbari Clubs in Nigeria and this was a sister institute.

Chemi-chemi is Swahili for a fountain; the name was meant as a symbol of the freshness and rebirth of creative talent. Mphahlele directed its activities for three years, during which he ran writers' workshops in secondary schools and took theater groups to perform in the provinces. There was an art gallery in the Centre and a theater stage for experimental African theater and music.

The year 1967 found Mphahlele teaching African, Afro-American, and Caribbean literature at the University of Colorado in Denver, U.S.A. He also began to prepare for a doctoral degree there which he gained in June, 1968. From 1968 to 1970 he was associate professor of literature at the University of Zambia in Lusaka, after which he returned to Denver.

Thus, wherever he went, Mphahlele continued to teach English literature and to organize cultural activities. In Africa, working at what he describes as "grassroot level," he found it rewarding to work "towards the integration of social and cultural goals with the aims and systems of education."[8] The teaching of literature, he found, could be an organic part of the learning process. It was more difficult for him to fit into the American system, with its long line of continuity. He felt a sense of irrelevance as far as cultural goals were concerned. With interest increasing in African affairs, however, he soon must have become aware of the role in American education that he could perform.

Mphahlele published two more collections of short stories, containing the last short fiction he has written to date: *The Living and Dead*, published in 1961 by the Ministry of Education, Ibadan Western Region, as a special publication of the periodical *Black Orpheus*, and *In Corner B*, published in 1967 in Nairobi by the East Africa Publishing House. After that, his main literary output, until his novels, consisted of essays and critical writing. He began to become known as an authority on African literature and allied subjects, and was invited to contribute articles to publications and help edit journals such as the *East Africa Journal*, the *Journal of the New African Literature and the Arts*, and *Research in African Literatures*, as well as to attend and address conferences. His opinions were respected wherever he went. When he paid his first visit to England he was feted by his publishers, Messrs. Faber and Faber, and by his literary agents, Messrs. Curtis Brown.

He first participated in a conference in Accra in December, 1958, where he represented the African National Congress. His speech, he tells us in his report,[9] moved his audience to tears. His first visit to the United States came in July, 1960, for a conference of the American Society of Culture in Philadelphia. By 1962 he was sufficiently well known to be asked to preside over a Conference of African Writers at Makerere University in Kampala, Uganda. In

March, 1963, he attended a conference at Dakar, which he had organized on behalf of the Congress for Cultural Freedom. It was continued in Freetown in April of that year and discussed matters close to his heart, the introduction of African writing in university studies. By 1967 he was recognized as an authority and invited to act as chairperson of the African-Scandinavian Writers' Conference held at Häselby Castle outside Stockholm. Per Wästberg, a participating Scandinavian writer and himself an authority on African writing, describes Mphahlele as a superb chairperson, firmly but gently steering a stormy meeting through to its end, knowing everybody, but favoring no one, joking mildly, knowing more about the subject than most, but not pushing his own opinion.[10]

II   The Living and Dead and Other Stories

The stories in the collection *The Living and Dead and Other Stories* were all written in South Africa, although they were published in Ibadan by the Nigerian Ministry of Education in 1961, during the time when Mphahlele was teaching there. The slim, soft-covered volume is attractively illustrated by the black South African artist, Peter Clarke. Most of the stories had appeared before, the title story in *Africa South* (January - March issue, 1958), "The Suitcase" in *Black Orpheus* (October, 1958), "The Master of Doornvlei" in *Fighting Talk* in 1957. "The Woman" and "The Woman Walks Out" are very similar to chapters in *Down Second Avenue*.

The collection no longer has the autobiographical unity of *Down Second Avenue* or the unity of background of the "Lesane" stories and the stories in *Man Must Live*. All are based in South Africa, but the background varies. Some take place in the city, in the offices of lawyers and welfare organizations where Mphahlele spent some of his working days; another on a farm, about which he learnt while reporting for *Drum;* in only two instances is there a township background.

More white people appear in these stories than in his previous fiction; in two stories, in fact, they are the main characters. Except in the two sketches from *Down Second Avenue,* black people are shown in relation to the white world around them. They are servants, farm laborers, and city workers. Most of the plots concern conflict between black and white. The stories represent the protest stage of Mphahlele's writing. Although they were written in South Africa, he selected them a year or two after he had left. They must thus be considered as reflecting his state of mind at the time: bitter, disillusioned. The race theme is predominant. Characters are black or white in character, according to the color of their skin. "It would be nice," one of them in the title story says, "if one could just take a label out of the pocket and tack it on the lapel of a man's coat."[11] This Mphahlele does figuratively in several of the stories.

III *"The Living and Dead"*

The title story of the collection, "The Living and Dead," suffers from the same disadvantage as most stories written in protest against a system. Plot and character have little chance to develop, either spontaneously toward a pleasing work of art, or according to the laws of probability and the principles of psychology. They have to suit a purpose extraneous to fiction. The theme thus becomes illustrative of the writer's outlook rather than arising out of it.

Here, the white master - black servant relationship is the theme. The white man has built up iron walls in himself as a means of protection against any feelings for the black man. Eventually he does realize that his servant is human, but decides that it will be better to "continue treating him as a name, not as another human being," and to let him "continue to be a machine to work for him."[12]

In his protest writing Mphahlele's compassion for humanity leads to a flaw in understanding. He cannot envisage others not sharing his deep feeling for his fellowmen and can thus attribute the racial feelings of the South African white man only to guilt. Sadly, the major reason for racial hatred is fear, and for lack of understanding pure indifference. In the South African context the events and characters of "The Living and Dead" are impossible.

The main character is a white man, the Afrikaner Stoffel Visser. The only Afrikaners, or Boers as he prefers to call them, Mphahlele knew at this time were petty government officials on the other side of a counter, policemen, and employers with whom he had little personal contact and whom he regarded as "machines." Now, in order to portray them in fiction, Mphahlele had to animate such machines and visualize these cold and unfriendly people at home. The result is caricature. Today, Mphahlele is fully aware of the problem — and he tells us that he does not care! In the revised version of *The African Image* he says:

I used to worry that, because we see each other through a key hole — we blacks and whites in South Africa — I cannot portray the character of a white man in the round. Often when I have turned the white stereotype round to look at it from another angle, I have tugged or pushed fiercely so that the figure came back to the initial position. I missed what I had thought I might find. Because I didn't want to see it, because it was a strain on my patience, because my anger was against me . . .

I get to know him [boss or foreman] only as an adult who carries on him the badge of his tribe, and, perhaps more than he will ever realize, the burden and even curse of being white. I used to worry that there is so much else I do not know about this symbol of power, prosperity, privilege; that gunslinging, baton-swinging cop; this ogre sitting judgement over a black law breaker. I wanted my portrait of him in my fiction to be fuller so I myself could begin to understand him. Over the last ten years I have ceased to care. It is not worth the trouble. The white man's inhumanity in South Africa has proved that much to me. To feel his muscle in real life is to understand him. And that seems enough for now. I will still enjoy engineering my own poetic justice against him. If any critic tells me my white characters are caricatures or only monsters, he is welcome to the opinion.[13]

Perhaps, if Mphahlele had felt this at the time of writing "The Living and Dead," he might have relaxed and allowed his white men a place as a force, as he did in the *Drum* stories and in *Down Second Avenue*. When a white man becomes the pivot of a short story, however, this attitude becomes difficult to tolerate. It also contradicts Mphahlele's opinion of other writers. When he speaks of Joseph Conrad's *Almayer's Folly* and *An Outcast of the Islands*, he says: "Conrad's greatness as an artist lies in his disinclination to recognize boundaries in human character when he writes about Malays and Arabs."[14] Speaking about William Faulkner's *Light in August:* "This is not just a 'race relations story,' even within the narrow boundaries of Deep South life with its parochial and stock attitudes. Joe is not just a black man whose problems are externalized in terms of racial discrimination."[15] And about E. M. Forster's *Passage to India:* "What message there is in *Passage to India* is subtly conveyed: it never, as in Paton's *Cry, the Beloved Country* and so much of other fiction, supersedes character."[16] He concludes: "Aziz, Joe Christman, Conrad's Nina, and Aissa are memorable literary creations because they cannot be hewn and carved to fit into the frame of local politics; because they are endowed with the human characteristics which have permanence and which suffer and endure historical change."[17]

These comments appear both in the original and the revised version of his book *The African Image*, and may thus be accepted as

Mphahlele's view of race in literature. In the old version of *The African Image* he continues his comments as follows:

English fiction in South Africa is obsessed with race relations. The *plot* is the thing, and as race conflicts provide innumerable facile plots, we are in for a gold rush; and so character counts for little or nothing. In fact, I rather suspect that we, both black and white, unconsciously want to maintain the *status quo* so as to delay as long as we can the coming of the day when we as writers shall be faced with the greater responsibility of inventing plot and reconstructing character in broader human perspective.[18]

Although this passage is less emphatic in the revised version, these comments tacitly condemn some of his own stories, such as "The Living and Dead" and one or two others in this collection.

Not only does Stoffel Visser remain an inanimate concept, but he is such a mass of contradictions that he cannot even function as a symbol. His friend Doppie Fourie speaks of Stoffel's superior intellect. He sees him as full of mental energy, a complex human being with an artist's face, perhaps even a genius. Admittedly Doppie, as his name implies (a *dop* is Afrikaans for a tot of liquor) is a drunkard, but his estimate must be taken seriously, since Stoffel seeks out his companionship. Moreover, the "Christian Protestant Party" has made Stoffel secretary of its Social Affairs Commission. There is nothing in what Stoffel says, thinks, or does throughout the story to substantiate Doppie's or the Party's high opinion of the man. Stoffel is bigoted: "We haven't much time to waste looking at both sides of the question" — he speaks in clichés: "what's to happen to white civilization?" — he is conceited: "If I feel pressed to speak you must listen, like it or not."[19] In spite of the bigotry ascribed to him, in spite of the stock attitudes that we are told his mother and father, his brothers, his friends, his schoolmasters, his university professors, and all the others who claimed him as their own had planted in him; in spite of all this, Mphahlele would have us believe that this negrophobe realizes the injustice that is being done to the black man, to the extent of finding it necessary to steel himself against the echo of hate and vengeance from the past.

Stoffel's hatred of the black man is his hobby. As secretary of the Commission, he has spent weeks preparing a report for the Party's representative in Parliament, asking for the number of servants in each household to be reduced. Ironically, the report fails to reach the

representative in time because Stoffel's own servant, Jackson, was
not there to wake him early enough.

In the course of the story Stoffel is made aware of Jackson as a
human being. At first his absence is an inconvenience. Then a
railway worker comes to the door with a letter he found on the
tracks, written to Jackson by his dying father. Next to arrive is
Virginia, Jackson's wife, who sobs out her distress at his disappearance, just on the day when he had promised to take the
children to the zoo. Stoffel gets into his car and drives five miles to
the nearest police station, but in vain. Questions now keep "bobbing
up from somewhere in his soul." He has apparently stopped thinking
of the "kafirs swarming over our suburbs," entering white homes
and sleeping with white girls. Instead, he sees "Virginia's pathetic
look, her roundabout unpunctuated manner of saying things."[20]

Returning from his office the next day, Stoffel finds Jackson in his
room, his face swollen and bandaged. He has been beaten up by the
police, who taunted him for reading a book on the train. Stoffel calls
a doctor for him, an unprecedented action. Jackson and his family
have become "human flesh and blood and heart and mind" to him.
But suddenly he remembers that it is his duty to be a white man,
before he is a human being. Mphahlele spells out the moral of the
story for the reader just before the end. If only the white man gave
himself time "to clear the whole muddle," then he would hear the
"cry of shame" and black people would become "human flesh and
blood and heart and mind."[21] Instead, Stoffel chooses to let Jackson
continue to be "a machine to work for him"[22] and to do what he considers his duty as a responsible white man, in this case to hand in the
Commission's report.

The title is somewhat puzzling though it must necessarily be of
importance since Mphahlele uses it as the title for the collection.
There is only one "dead" in the story, an unknown man who is
trampled to death at the railway station by two converging crowds.
The railway worker who tells Stoffel of the incident describes the
crowds as being like one river going against another. The dead man
may be meant as a symbol for the questions that Stoffel does not
want to think about, those concerning black men as human beings,
some living and some dead. Or else the dead may be the disembodied voices Stoffel hears coming down through the centuries,
echoing hate and vengeance, while the living are the voices of the
black men and women of flesh and blood and heart and mind.

The little action there is in the story tends to stall. The style of

writing lacks the usual animation. The white men's dialogue, which
covers the first few pages, is stilted to the point of being embarrassing; for example:

"Look here, Doppie Fourie, *ou kêrel*, you deceived yourself to think I want
to hear myself talk."
"I didn't mean that, Stoffel. But of course you have always been very clever.
I envy you for your brains. Anyhow, I don't promise to be an obedient
listener tonight. I just want to drink."[23]

IV *"We'll Have Dinner at Eight"*

Equally unsatisfactory both as a piece of fiction and as a study in
race relations is "We'll Have Dinner at Eight." Miss Pringle, the
principal white character, is a little more plausible than Stoffel, at
least in so far as we learn to know her. Her life, too, seems to center
around her feelings for the black man. Miss Pringle makes "a conscious effort to win non-white friends," not because she has "abundant sympathy for the needy," as her testimonials state, but because
she likes to have "a crowd of Blacks hovering over her admiringly,"
and because it is more fun working with them than with whites.
"Too independent, that's the way with Whites."[24] Miss Pringle —
we never learn her first name — is therefore a woman apparently not
accepted by her group, a spinster, whose superiors in the social
welfare organization where she works, in spite of her glowing
testimonials, describe her confidentially as "a trifle tiresome, but
hardworking," "a little overbearing, but conscientious," or "a
likeable person, but a queer fish." We are left in no doubt how we
are to feel about Miss Pringle right from the beginning. Her efforts
to win black friends were undertaken "with an eternal smile on her
lips." Miss Pringle is hypocritical, self-deceiving, and sexually
frustrated. Mzondi, who comes to the welfare institution to learn a
trade, appears to Miss Pringle as an answer to her needs. He is poor
and crippled, and therefore helpless and in need of her care; and he
is a man whose "pathetic beautiful lips" and "steady eyes, almost ex-
pressionless"[25] intrigue her. To befriend him becomes a passion with
her.

Miss Pringle is utterly repulsive. Mphahlele may have intended to
arouse our sympathy for her, but his dislike of a type prevented him
from creating a character. The irony of her murder by the man she
befriends therefore fails to appear tragic, and the theme of misunderstanding between black and white falls flat.

Mzondi dreams of building a beautiful house and fetching his little daughter from the country to live with him. For this dream he has
stolen two thousand pounds and allowed the police to beat him
savagely in their attempt to discover its hiding place. As a result, he
suffered a partial paralysis.

Although Mzondi senses Miss Pringle's need for him whenever
she bends over him to show him how to operate a machine, he does
not understand her and merely wishes she would leave him alone.
Four times he has refused her invitation to a meal at her apartment.
When the action of the story starts, however, a policeman enters her
office on some official business unconnected with Mzondi, but it
makes him think that her invitation is a plot to get him drunk and
reveal where he has hidden the two thousand pounds. He accepts
the invitation with murder in his heart. The deed is done after the
sherry, as Miss Pringle bends down to massage Mzondi's knee at his
request.

A young patrolman, alerted by the night watchman of the apartment building, who saw the couple enter the elevator, goes up to the
apartment, hoping to catch them in bed, a crime of immorality
between black and white under South African law. Instead he finds
Miss Pringle alone, her crushed head a sodden mess. Mzondi escapes
in the chase that follows, but the exertion is too much for him and he
collapses and dies.

This is one of Mphahlele's few short stories with sexual overtones.
The irony of the contrapuntal themes is promising, the spinster who
hides her unconscious sexual longings behind the cloak of a do-
gooder and the lack of comprehension of the cripple to whom
anyone white represents an unjust law and therefore danger. There
is neither tragedy nor pathos, however, partly because of the poorly
motivated murder — if Mzondi was afraid Miss Pringle would make
him drunk and drag his secret out of him all he had to do was to stay
away from her dinner — but mainly because of the lack of sympathy
for or even interest in the two protagonists. No real attempt is made
to explore either Mzondi's or Miss Pringle's human motives. These
are merely hinted at and are not developed to the point where compassion can envelop both contenders.

What is the message of the story? There is condemnation of a legal
system which is prejudiced against the black man. Mzondi is acquitted of the crime of theft he did commit, but the judge refuses to
believe the story of his beating by the police in spite of the evidence.
The conclusion one draws from the story is one of hopelessness in

racial relations. If white shows signs of friendliness toward black, white's motives are suspect; black cannot accept such friendship under any terms, since it cannot be trusted.

V "The Master of Doornvlei"

This story was probably written before the others in the collection, at about the same time as the "Lesane" stories. Here, too, we have a confrontation, but this time the labels are less distinct, the protagonists more complex. In the country the situation is different in that the bond between white farmer and black laborers is a more essential one than between master and domestic servant or welfare worker and her charge. Miss Pringle saw only pity in her relationship, Stoffel was aware only of his comforts, but Sarel Britz, the owner of the farm Doornvlei, knows that it is necessary to establish a workable relationship. He stresses repeatedly that he is just to his laborers. Although Sarel is no more sympathetic a character than the others, he is not merely the representative of a type.

Sarel and his mother live together on the farm. To her the head of family and farm is supreme. If "your father himself said so," there was an end to it. Sarel's father, during his lifetime, had thought of his black laborers as children, but Sarel has been to the city to study agriculture, and he knows that the father-child relationship is a white man's myth. He treats his men justly because he needs them, but added to this is a new element, fear. They are no longer children, he assures his mother. How are they grown up, she wants to know? Sarel goes and stands right in front of her. "Yes, Ma," he says, "they're fully grownup; some of them cleverer and wiser than a lot of us Whites. Their damned patience makes them all the more dangerous."[26]

The laborers are protesting against the actions of the Rhodesian black foreman, Mfukeri, who whips them in spite of Sarel's instructions to desist. Mfukeri drives the laborers beyond their physical endurance, and when a ten-year-old boy dies of pneumonia after being made to work in the rain, the men ask for his dismissal. They are led by Tau Rathebe, a refugee from Johannesburg. Sarel listens, but when Rathebe imposes an ultimatum on him he cannot tolerate this from a black man. Sarel dismisses Rathebe and tells the workers that the foreman is being given a last chance. The laborers are unhappy at the outcome, but they are helpless because they cannot leave. "No," Rathebe tells them, "The police will take you as soon as you leave here. You can't go from one farm to another without a trek-pass,"[27] he reminds them, and the passe? would not be issued to them without Sarel's consent.

As time goes on, the farm prospers, but Sarel's fear increases. He constantly reminds his men that he is just, but he becomes sterner and more exacting. He is afraid that the workers will be drawn to better-paying jobs in the towns, or that they will rise against the farmers. The more he grows afraid, the more dependent he becomes on his foreman. Yet he also fears the foreman and catches the nuances of diminishing deference in his attitude toward him.

The conflicts culminate in a confrontation, not between Sarel and Mfukeri on the one hand and the workers on the other, but between white and black as represented by Sarel and Mfukeri. The laborers are indifferent. Sarel becomes aware of the threat to his authority when Mfukeri's bull engages in battle with Sarel's pedigree stallion. "Master and foreman watched, each feeling that he was entangled in this strife between their animals; more so than they dared to show outwardly. Sarel Britz bit his lower lip as he watched the rage of the bull. He seemed to see scalding fury in the very slime that came from the mouth of the bull to mix with the earth."[28] When the bull gores the stallion, Mfukeri feels overwhelming triumph. But it cannot be allowed to last. Sarel gives Mfukeri the choice of shooting his bull or leaving. The story ends:

Mfukeri did not answer. They both knew the moment had come. He stood still and looked at Britz. Then he walked off, and coaxed his bull out of the premises.

"I gave him a choice," Sarel said to his mother, telling her the whole story.

"You shouldn't have, Sarel. He has worked for us these fifteen years."

Sarel knew he had been right. As he looked out of the window to the empty paddock, he was stricken with grief. And then he was glad. He had got rid of yet another threat to his authority.

But the fear remained.[29]

There are still no fully portrayed white people in this story. We are made to understand Sarel's motives in the handling of his labor force. He is contrasted in his attitude toward the black man with the older generation, represented by his mother, but we know nothing else of their relationship; we cannot picture Sarel loving, eating, sleeping, and growing old. Mfukeri is merely a force poised against him, with ambition as his only drive.

The symbolism of the story is forced. Mphahlele seems impatient

with his rural background. In his fiction he rarely uses nature either
descriptively or symbolically. It is again the mass of people that he
describes most effectively. The story opens in a mud and grass
church house where the congregation watch the elderly soft-spoken
preacher closely, so as not to miss any of his words, one or two older
women screwing up their faces in their effort to follow. Abstractedly
they watch a bird flitting from rafter to rafter, trapped in the church.
The bird represents the helplessness of the people entrapped in a
labor system where they have no redress against wrongs. A little boy
rescues the bird when it flies into the window and drops. He leaves
the bird under an empty can when he is called from the church to
work in the rain. The bird dies and the little boy succumbs to
pneumonia. His death triggers off the action of the story; the people
have been driven too far and rebel.

Animals symbolize the end as well as the beginning of the action,
but the battle between the beasts merely reflects the lack of tension
in the confrontation between the humans. The laborers watch with
little interest; there is no sense of climax. As always, violence is
abhorrent to Mphahlele and he hurries over the scene.

VI   *"The Woman"* and *"The Woman Walks Out"*

The remaining stories do not feature white characters. The above
two stories are based on incidents in *Down Second Avenue* featuring
Ma-Lebona, here known as 'Madira. Entire sections coincide, but
the stories are more coherently organized so that they can stand
alone. They were published in periodicals before the appearance of
Down Second Avenue, but may have been extracts from the
manuscript. They show once more the thin dividing line between
Mphahlele's autobiographical writing and his fiction.

The incidents involving Ma-Lebona are among the most amusing
in *Down Second Avenue*, and typical of the writing that gives the
autobiography much of its appeal. 'Madira's description of the
woman who is too lazy to go out and buy milk and thus squeezes out
her own milk into her husband's tea is not just told for its humorous
effect, but brings 'Madira's earthiness into sharp relief. We also
learn that she herself was so clean that she often had meat taken out
of boiling water to be rewashed. There emerges a wonderful portrait
of a snob, contrasted in *Down Second Avenue* with a woman like
Mphahlele's mother, who, on a servant's wages, quietly put her son
through high school. 'Madira complains of the privations she endures and shudders to think of what she will do when her children go

to the university. However, they fail to pass the third-last high school form.

'Madira's first husband left her after three years' marriage, the second after two years of "nagging, spying and scandal." Her third man did not marry her, and also deserted her. She was left with a daughter and a son from the last two partners. It was then, that "having thus failed to run husbands," 'Madira decided "to use all her genius (which she believed she had) in being a mother-in-law."[30] Her own daughter gains her independence early by marrying, moving out, and firmly ignoring interference. Joel, the son, however, is subservient to her and allows his wife to be bullied. The first daughter-in-law stands it for just over a year, the second prospective bride is warned in time; she fails to turn up for the wedding. We hear an echo of Mphahlele's theme that man must live. "Come, come, my son," 'Madira comforts him, as her son lays his head on her lap and cries like a child who has lost his best toy: "This world can be a paradise, and it can be hell. But we must not give in so."[31] But the theme here is used ironically, since 'Madira is unaware that she is the one who created the hell for her son and brought about his humiliation in being stood up at the church door through her foolish social aspirations. This element of irony, present in almost all of the stories, turns the funny incident of the autobiography into a full rounded short story.

In "The Woman Walks Out" the pen-portraits of 'Madira and her son Joel are continued. Even if we had not met Joel before, we would have no difficulty in picturing him immediately, standing at his mother's sick bed, answering "yes Mamma" to all her complaints. Even the pastor is a little afraid of 'Madira. "The Woman Walks Out" is the story of 'Madira's death. Conscious of her self-imposed social status to the last, she startles her neighbors one day by declaring that when she dies she wants to be buried in the old cemetery which is well-kept, lined with avenues of trees, and full of statuettes and tombstones, whereas the new cemetery is merely covered with coarse grass. She also prepares an elaborate shroud. Ironically, she dies while visiting in the country, and though Joel brings the shroud, the country folk refuse to bury her in it. Her last resting place is even more desolate than the new cemetery in her town. With compassion and sympathy for this woman — selfish, vain, and eccentric though she is, but always passionately alive — Mphahlele spares her the final indignity of knowing that this will happen. She collapses and dies without regaining consciousness.

VII   *"The Suitcase"*

The ironic twists of life are also the subject of "The Suitcase." Here the irony is a little too obvious to make the plot plausible, although, ironically, Mphahlele says in *Down Second Avenue* that it is in essence a true story, told to him by his wife about an incident in Sophiatown. In the 'Madira stories the irony arises purely out of the character, whereas in "The Suitcase" the events play a more active role. Timi, unemployed and desperate, is waiting for "sheer naked chance" to find a way of bringing a present to his wife on Old Year's Eve. He finds it on a bus when a woman passenger apparently forgets to take her suitcase. Another passenger sees Timi take it and reports him to the police. He is caught, and at the police station repeatedly swears that the case is his. But he has played with fate and lost. The case contains a dead baby.

Although unlikely, the plot is tight and the characters plausible. Timi, first revealed in a short series of events told without comment, which flash through his mind as he sits in the sun, is the typical town African. He is contemptuous of the white people whom he asks for jobs because he knows that in a normal society they would be his inferiors. There is a tiny typist who tells him "You're too big, John,"[32] and then goes on with her typing, clouding her white face with cigarette smoke. He chuckles to himself when he recalls a pudgy man with fat white cheeks and small blinking eyes, who refuses to pay a living wage.

The stage for the action is set skillfully right at the beginning. Timi is sitting on the pavement on a hot afternoon, day-dreaming about a chance to get rich which might present itself one of these days, and which he would make sure not to miss. An insect flies into his nose and makes him sneeze. As always, description is in terms of movement. Timi now sees the scene before him through the tears that fill his eyes, and this makes the traffic dance before him. The events unfold and the expectancy is heightened. The suitcase is introduced early in the story and its ultimate importance hinted at. The scenes are vivid. We hear and see the crowd in the bus, good humored and full of noisy laughter, even during the argument as to whether the suitcase is Timi's. "Oh, leave him alone," comes a voice from one part of the bus, answering one in another quarter, "only one man saw the girl come in with a suitcase, and only one man says it is his. One against one. Let him keep what he has, the case. Let the other man keep what he has, the belief that it belongs to the girl."

There is a roar of laughter. "The argument melted in the air of a happy New Year, of revelry and song."[33] This is followed by the rising sound of angry noises, which whirl and circle around Timi in a savage, menacing crescendo when the hunt for him has begun.

The denouement is handled well and with the necessary tension. Timi is standing in a small room as two constables start to unpack the suitcase, holding up pieces of torn clothing for Timi to identify as his wife's belongings. He senses their cold amusement and feels that something is wrong. Finally one of the constables points to an object and says: *"And is this also your wife's?"* glaring at Timi with aggressive eyes. Timi stretches his neck to see. The story ends simply:

It was a ghastly sight. A dead baby that could not have been born more than twelve hours before. A naked, white, curly-haired image of death. Timi gasped and felt sick and faint. They had to support him to the counter to make a statement. He told the truth. He knew he had gambled with chance; the chance that was to cost him eighteen months' hard labour.[34]

The theme of this story is not the vagaries of fate, but the choices man has before him. Timi confuses the two component elements of chance. He speaks of taking advantage of a chance and of being provided with a lucky chance as though it were the same thing. It is this confusion between chance as fate and chance with an option that leads to his downfall. His wife is aware of the true meaning of chance and this forms a basis for her optimistic view of life. She says: "Tomorrow's sun must rise, Timi. It rises for everyone. It may have its fortunes," but "I will make a little fire, Timi. Our sages say even where there is no pot to boil there should be fire."[35] Timi, on the other hand, thinks that an external power presents opportunities and will reward you if you seize them. In this case a suitcase has fallen into his hands, and since he has been clever enough to keep it, even at the risk of being caught, it is bound to contain valuables. "It is so heavy, there must be. It couldn't be otherwise. Else why had Providence been so kind to him so far? Surely the spirits of his ancestors had pity on him; with a sick wife and hungry children."[36] He is torn between a feeling of conventional guilt at taking what is not his and indignation that people should interfere with what has obviously been granted him by Providence. Only at the end does he face the truth. Chance is a gamble; there is nothing outside yourself working for you. And so he tells the police the truth.

Timi may not have the stature of a hero; his choice is not a matter of life and death and his downfall only an eighteen months' jail sentence. Nevertheless, this is tragedy in the classical sense. However far-fetched the plot, the theme arises spontaneously out of plot and characters, and the story is perhaps Mphahlele's most successful piece of fiction. He showed the well-known South African writer, Nadine Gordimer, some of his work in manuscript one day, and she became most enthusiastic about this particular story. She insisted on submitting it to *New World Writing*, where it appeared in the seventh Mentor Selection in 1955 in company with Heinrich Böll, Elizabeth Jennings, Dylan Thomas, and others.

VIII   *"He and the Cat"*

This story, the most widely reprinted of the stories in this collection, was written later than the others and is more subtle than the rest. There is no sequence of events. The narration concerns only the thoughts of the speaker, developing an impressionistic reflection of several concurrent abstract sequences.

While sitting in a lawyer's waiting room, the narrator is going over an unnamed problem in his mind, rehearsing what he plans to tell the lawyer. At the same time he is aware of the waiting room, of its walls and ceilings and furniture, and of the people in it. His very concentration brings other thoughts to his mind; the previous night's adventures, his girl friend. His eyes jump from a picture of a cat to a man sealing envelopes, sitting beneath it, and to a fly on the wall, and then out through the window to the tops of the tall buildings of the city.

The narrator is a passive figure to whom the kaleidoscope unfolds. Deliberately we are not told the nature of his problem. The objects he sees are as humdrum and common as possible. The narrator, who refers to himself by the pronoun "you" used impersonally, is as it were suspended in time, place, and thought. "You seemed to float on the stagnant air in the room, but a creature in the no-time of feeling and thought."[37] The man sealing envelopes speaks in meaningless aphorisms, the waiting clients of the lawyer discuss events common to all, "babbling away over things that did not concern them . . . pretending they had suspended moments of anxiety."[38] It is the heat of the afternoon, the closeness of the room, and its drab appearance, which complete the sense of suspension from living.

The clients are called in one by one and finally the narrator is left alone with the man and the picture of the cat. His heart gives a hard beat as his mind switches back to reality, to the problem that has brought him here. Then something else happens and this time his mind is jolted into confused activity. Understanding follows. The man sitting under the picture of the cat, performing his monotonous task of sealing envelopes and muttering his meaningless remarks, bends down to pick up an envelope, and it becomes evident that he is completely blind. For a moment the narrator sees him as flat and without depth, "too flat even to be hindered by the heat, the boredom of sitting for hours doing the same work, by too many or too few people coming. An invincible pair, he and the cat glowering at him, scorning our shames and hurts and the heat, seeming to hold the key to the immediate imperceptible and the most remote unforeseeable. . . ."[39]

The blind man becomes a symbol of mindlessness, of the Kafkaesque rift with reality which emanates from the room. But this is an illusion, an absurdity. Then it is over and the narrator returns to the business of living. He goes in to see the lawyer and tells him his business.

The style of this story is in complete accord with its contents. The short staccato sentences, the emphasis on verbs and nouns of action, the graphic presentation of cameos in the waiting room — the clients are described as "those dolls that have to be bowled out at a merry-go-round fair," and their troubles as "eddies and bubbles bursting on a heat wave"[40] — form an ironic contrast to the sense of suspended animation.

Some of the stories eventually enjoyed the wider readership they deserved. "The Living and Dead" appeared in an East German anthology, *Following the Sun* (Berlin: Seven Seas Books, 1960); "He and the Cat" was published in *The Classic* in 1963 (i,1.), and incorporated in anthologies collected by Ulli Beier *(Black Orpheus)* and by Nadine Gordimer and Lionel Abrahams *(South African Writing To-day)*. "The Woman" appeared in *Purple Renoster* and "The Woman Walks Out" in *Standpunte*. "The Suitcase," as mentioned earlier, appeared in *New World Writing*.

CHAPTER 5

In Corner B

M PHAHLELE'S last collection of short stories, *In Corner B*, was published by the East African Publishing House in Nairobi in 1967. Again several stories had been published elsewhere, the title story in *The Classic*, "The Coffee-Cart Girl" and "Down the Quiet Street" in *Drum* (January, 1956), and "Across Down Stream" also in *Drum* (August, 1955). "Man Must Live," "The Living and Dead," "The Master of Doornvlei," and "He and the Cat" had appeared in earlier collections. The only new stories were "The Barber of Bariga," "Grieg on a Stolen Piano" (which contains incidents from *Down Second Avenue*), the title story, "A Ballad of Oyo," "A Point of Identity," and "Mrs. Plum."

As an African rather than a South African writer, Mphahlele very likely now felt that he must face the responsibility he mentions in *The African Image* of inventing plot and constructing characters outside the ready-made plots provided by the racial question. Yet only two of the stories are based outside South Africa, although Mphahlele had now been away for ten years. With South Africa as a background, the racial question is of course predominant, but in at least one of the new stories he goes far more deeply into the problems of racial attitudes than he has done before. The two non-South African stories show a certain unease. Mphahlele found it difficult to become emotionally involved in Nigerian affairs, while at the same time the enforced passivity probably made him unhappy.

I "The Barber of Barigo"

Passivity in the face of the turmoil around him is the theme of this story. Here Mphahlele expresses his reaction to the currents and cross-currents of life in an independent African state through his main character, the barbar Anofi, a passive man who refuses to become emotionally involved in his surroundings.

To Anofi, people are heads with hair to be cut, and among these he feels at ease. By the nature of his profession, he listens to the confidences of his clients as he ploughs through their hair with his clippers. Unlike his father, however, he does not become involved. The old man sits in his son's shop, entertaining the customers with funny stories and more often than not starting an argument. Anofi never wants to stir up things. He says very little himself, always looks unruffled, and seems "incapable of nervous tension, of anger or malice."[1]

He witnesses an accident involving a white couple in a car and a black cyclist, and is asked by the white woman who was at fault, but again he refuses to become involved. The world is a large place for him, with plenty of room for everyone. He knows, for instance, that his wife is beautiful, but she seldom "leaps into his field of awareness."[2] When a blind beggar or blind women with children on their backs would "wail their incantations to Allah with heartrending effect," Anofi's father's jaws "pounded harder on the kola nut and, with the aid of the tongue, drew air through the side teeth to hiss his bewilderment and pride."[3] Anofi himself, however, would give something quickly and tell them to go away.

But such withdrawal, Mphahlele makes it clear, is reprehensible. No one is entitled to go through life as a spectator as Anofi does, ignoring the throbbing world around him, the cavalcade of drum-beating masqueraders, of weddings and funeral processions that pass by the window of the barbershop, and the blaring, pulsating noise emanating from the radio shop across the road. "Deep-deep down in the pit of his stomach"[4] something stirs in Anofi. That is why he does not send the beggars away altogether empty-handed. A cord inside him quivers, yet he continues to ignore the warning signs.

The first head we see under the clippers is Bashiru's, that of a man of property who has several wives and still chases after the girls. One day a message comes to Anofi that Bashiru has died while attending a wedding and that he must come and shave his head to prepare him for burial, according to the religious cult to which Bashiru belonged. As Anofi is about to finish the job, his clippers strike against something hard. He shaves around the object until it emerges. He has found the cause of death, a large nail driven into the man's head. He shouts out his discovery, then dashes from the house without waiting for the reaction, and walks home. On his way he meets Okeke, a man who had told him two days earlier that Bashiru was stealing his — Okeke's — wife. Okeke now admits to Anofi that he killed Bashiru, for he knows that Anofi will tell no one. "Why?" Anofi wants to know, and Okeke replies: "Becos Bashiru he don' make lawve for you wife, too, idi-awt! Wake op! She waitin' to tell you for house. See you nex' tomorrow."[5] It is then that Anofi begins to understand what he has been evading. He sees his wife's beauty for what it is. Suddenly the world around him seems small and over-crowded, the radio music sets his nerves quivering. He decides to pack his entire household and go away.

Mphahlele has no difficulty in absorbing the atmosphere of a new milieu. His ear for language and accents, cultivated in the babel of a Transvaal black township, enables him to produce dialogue with a vernacular flavor. He enjoys depicting the scenes in the barbershop, the pride the barber takes in his work. "As his clippers nibbled down the slopes, he seemed conscious of his skill. And his client relaxed the more, conscious of his physical ease and the good job being done of his cut."[6] It is the craftsman admiring the craft of another, some-thing we often find in Mphahlele's fiction. Even the work of a railway trackman, in "Man Must Live," is described with loving care.

"The Barber of Bariga" begins humorously. Why, the barber wants to know, does his client need a new woman every month. "Bot you no be happy for your t'ree wive?" Bashiru replies: "Yes, bot I wan' be more happy. You know what *oyingbo* say: he say De more de merry merrier merriest."[7] Outwardly the characters are sketched with skill, some in minute detail. We can see Anofi's father clearly, chewing away at his kola nut, his jaws moving like a goat's. Yet one feels that Mphahlele, like Anofi, is not really involved in the life of the people in the story. As a result, the account seems suffused rather than neat and confined. It fails both to make a point and to uphold interest.

A negative idea, lack of involvement, is a very difficult and un-satisfying one to illustrate dramatically. In this story the drama of seduction and murder is seen thirdhand, through the eyes of a man who is incapable of strong feelings. The characters, too, are mere abstractions. Anofi personifies passivity and the others, the con-trasting father, the seducer and murderer, are only representative of their function, however clearly their external features are drawn. In-cidents such as the accident to the white couple add nothing to the story, and the end leaves one unsatisfied.

II "A Ballad of Oyo"

The only other story with a Nigerian background is "A Ballad of
Oyo." O. R. Dathorne and Willfried Feuser included this story in
their anthology, *Africa in Prose*, an interesting choice when they had
all of Mphahlele's short fiction and his autobiography at their dis-
posal at the time. Their collection sought to show that there is a
recognizable prose tradition in African writing, and they attempted
to give a coherent view of African prose. They had to admit,
however, that "A Ballad of Oyo" was a "curiosity" piece in this
respect because the author "just about manages to reach beyond the
surface of Nigerian life."[8] He was wrong, in fact, they point out, in
making Yoruba market women speak pidgin. They wonder whether
the evidence in this story that it is written by a foreigner — an expatriate — explodes the theory that that there is an underlying unity
in African literature. Mphahlele himself has a great deal to say about
this in his essays. He feels in theory that there *are* broad elements of
the African personality common to all societies on the continent. In
practice, however, his first intoxication with freedom, and the feeling of unity, as we have seen, soon gave way to disillusionment and
the conclusion that human cultures have stone walls. These early
attempts in fiction to penetrate the wall failed because he found it
impossible to identify.

The Yoruba markets of West Africa have fascinated both foreign
and local writers through the years. To Mphahlele, as to others, there
is poetry in the market that tingles and buzzes and groans, and never
ceases, come rain, come blood, come malaria; its roar and chatter
and laughter and exclamation and smells make a live symphony,
quite independent of the people milling around it; the women
behind the counters walk the black tarmac road to and from the
market, walking, riding the dawn, walking into sunrise, their bodies
twisting at the hip.

"A Ballad of Oyo" is the story of one of the women, Ishola, also
known as Mama-Jimi. Married to a man who beats her and does not
work, she has asked the president of the court of local authority to
hear her case against the husband. When the story opens, the husband has gone to the north to see his other wives, while Ishola sets
out for the market. She is caught in a rainstorm and collapses at the
side of the road. She loses the child she is carrying. A week later she
is back at the market, determined now to leave her husband and go
to her lover Lijadu. Lijadu is prepared to pay the bride price for
Ishola, but her husband, Balogun, and his father refuse and bribe the

president of the court not to hear the case. Ishola goes to see the president of the court and gives him a bribe of five pounds. After he has heard her story, he grants her her request and gives her back the bribe money. Ishola is now free to leave and join Lijadu. She does so, but when she hears of the death of her father-in-law, his last words a cry for Ishola and her children, she decides to go back home.

Mphahlele calls the story a ballad to emphasize the folk-tale element. He uses various devices to create the illusion of a tale by an observer who has fallen under the spell of the market. Words and phrases are repeated to simulate narrative verse, for example: "And so goes the story of Ishola, Ishola, who was called Mama-Jimi, a mother of three children,"[9] and "It was the week before only the week before when the rain caught the market women on the tarmac to the market. The sky burst and the rain caught the market women on the tarmac to market. The sky burst and the rain came down with power."[10]

These effects give the story the air of a tragic tale, something of importance. This, however, is not borne out by the story itself. Here we have a woman who is attractive, who is misused by her husband, and who decides to leave him for another man, but changes her mind when the call to traditional duty claims her. We never learn to know Ishola, and she thus fails to arouse our sympathy. Other characters are introduced to little purpose: Ishola's sister who encourages her to leave her husband, and the president of the court who accepts bribes but, for reasons not explained, hands them back.

The market, although ostensibly so important to the story as a background — it is the ballad of Oyo, the market of Oyo, not of Ishola and her problems — does not really become an integral part of it. The fact that Ishola sells vegetables and fruit there is irrelevant to what befalls her. There is no dirction in either plot or setting. Thus it is with relief that we turn back to the South African stories in the collection. The stories selected from previous collections and periodicals include some of Mphahlele's best, such as "He and the Cat," "Man Must Live," "Down the Quiet Street," and "The Coffee-Cart Girl."

III   *"Grieg on a Stolen Piano"*

This story is also Mphahlele's choice for inclusion in an anthology entitled *Modern African Stories*, which he compiled together with Ellis Ayitey Komey, published in 1964. The publishers, Faber and Faber, we are told, insisted that the editors include their own stories.

Speaking of the South African contributions, the editors of this collection describe them as always groping for a medium "whereby they and their own immediate audience. . .can come to terms with a world of physical and mental violence."[11] "Grieg on a Stolen Piano" is perhaps Mphahlele's most successful attempt in this respect. He reverts to a background in which he is most at home. Once again he draws heavily on his own life.

The main character, like Mphahlele, goes through harassing experiences before he gains his goal, though in this case the experiences are wider in range and more physical in nature. He runs away from his home in a rural community toward Pietersburg and works on a farm where the whole white family of the owner periodically sit on the stoop and watch the laborers being whipped. Escaping, he travels through thick bush, where Mphahlele's fear of nature, ingrained as a child, finds expression. The boy remembers, as he continues his terrifying journey, the stories to which he had so often listened at the communal fire-place. "Always the theme was that of man, helpless as he himself was in the bush or on a tree or in a rock cave on a hill, who was unable to ward off danger, to escape a terrible power that was everywhere around him. Something seemed to be stalking him all the time, waiting for the proper moment to pounce upon him."[12] There follows a period in backyards of white suburbia and in a black township. An aunt then tracks him down and gives him a home, and he begins regular schooling. His education ends in triumph when he returns home to his parents as a hero, a teacher.

Although many of the experiences of the main character as a young man are those of the young Mphahlele, their personalities are dissimilar. The man is the narrator's uncle, and the narrator is in his charge after his own father's death. The uncle as a middle-aged man portrays a member of Mphahlele's family; some of his children are recognizable as Mphahlele's cousins in their occupations today. It is the narrator whose character resembles that of Mphahlele in his youth, a lawyer's clerk with simple tastes, unsophisticated, but with his eyes and his heart open for the people and events around him.

The uncle stands for a certain light-hearted adaptability, which the narrator cannot emulate, but which he both envies and finds irritating. Under the morality of the black township, it is permissible to get the better of authority in any guise, since the black man is accustomed to finding authority on the other side of the color line. The nephew subscribes to more conventional ideas of ethics. "But we

don't do such things, Uncle!'' he gasps, when the uncle tells him he
has spoken to the judges in a beauty contest in which they are sponsoring an entrant. What things? the uncle wants to know. "Talking
to judges about a competition in which you have vested interests."
"Don't talk so pompously," the uncle replies, "You're talking
English. Let's talk Sotho. Now all I did. . ."[13] All he did was to pay
his respects to each judge with a bottle of whisky. Toward the end of
the story the uncle expresses his philosophy clearly. "We don't all
have the liver to join the Congress Movement. So we keep stealing
from the white man and lying to him and he does the same. This way
we can still feel some pride."[14]

The piano of the title is bought quite legitimately, but the uncle's
second wife, a shrewish woman, finds out that the seller had stolen it
and takes him to task. The uncle is amused. "She worries about a
stolen piano, . . . She forgets she sleeps between stolen sheets; every
bit of cutlery that goes into her mouth was stolen by the boys from
whom I bought it; her blouses are stolen goods, her stockings." And
then, looking at his nephew, he continues, "Don't we steal from each
other, lie to each other every day and know it, us and the whites?"[15]

The uncle reaches the top of his profession as inspector of schools,
as well as becoming an accomplished musician. Then his life begins
to deteriorate. But although he succumbs to drink, gambling, and
dishonesty — illicit buying of uncut diamonds — he never departs
from his own concept of integrity and pride. He will not, for instance, continue as a lay preacher after gambling on horses becomes
a passion with him. He explains in his forthright and humorous way:

"I can't keep up the lies. . . .There are people who can mix religion with
gambling and the other things, but I can't. And gamble I must. As Christ
never explained what a black man should do in order to earn a decent living
in this country, we can only follow our instincts. And if I cannot understand
the connection, it is not right for me to stand in the pulpit and pretend to
know the answer."[16]

He refuses to carry a white colleague's typewriter, or to call any
white man "baas."

"Grieg on a Stolen Piano" follows the earlier story "Man Must
Live" in the collection. Like its predecessor, it also tells of the
deterioration of a character, triggered off by circumstances beyond
his control, but intrinsically arising out of his character. In the case
of the uncle, it is his first wife's death in childbirth that sets him on

his downhill path. Like Zungu, however, he never loses faith in survival as a necessity, though he is more subtle and suave in the way he applies this to his own life.

The uncle is presented as a synthesis of the traditional and of Western civilization. He is an inspector of schools, but, when he feels that ill-luck is stalking him, he slaughters a goat, feasts on it with relatives, and buries the bones in the yard according to custom: "At such times his mind searched the mystery of fate, groping in some imaginary world where the spirits of his ancestors and that of his dead wife must be living, for a point of contact, for a line of communion."[17] When ill, he sometimes calls in a doctor and sometimes a witchdoctor. Sometimes he plays Grieg on the stolen piano, and sometimes he improvises on well-known African tunes.

The central plot is a very amusing one, following Mphahlele's often-used method of mixing humor with a serious or realistic theme. The uncle has a foolproof scheme for making money: he will get a pretty girl from the country and train her for a beauty contest. The scheme is not as harebrained as it sounds; the girl is a typical village girl, but no yokel — in fact, not very different from her town cousin. All she needs is for her "bodily movements" to take on a "city rhythm." "Mary Jane," as they decide to call her, discarding her own name of Tryphina, gradually acquires these "movements" with the help of an instructor. The nephew takes her to the movies and introduces her to his collection of jazz records. After six months they feel they now have "a presentable article of good healthy flesh, comportment and luscious charm."[18] Love also has its part in this satiric plot. The nephew falls in love with the girl, but, being high-minded and less versatile in his morality than his uncle, he could not "face the prospect of living with someone I had presumed to raise to a level of sophistication for reasons of money."[19]

The judges of the beauty contest, as we have seen, are bribed by the uncle, but unfortunately it is subsequently decided that the winner shall be chosen by popular vote. Mary Jane loses but does not mind; she runs off with the physical instructor who trained her. Neither does the uncle mind: he simply regards the affair as a match that is lost and cannot be replayed.

The nephew has learnt his lesson: his education in life from a man who grasps its essentials is complete. He had a feeling all along that he would be better off if the gamble did not pay out; thus he can accept with equanimity the loss of the girl for whom he thought himself too sophisticated, and can also accept his uncle for what he is worth as a man, no longer standing aloof to moralize. The story ends on a comical interchange between the uncle and aunt. The uncle is playing the piano, and his wife suggests that, for her part, since one cannot eat "kiriki (Grieg) with the stolen piano," he can take him and his favorite African composer and put them in the lavatory bucket. "What do you do with your aunt, neph' " the uncle asks, "if she does not understand Grieg and cannot like Mohapeloa?" "If you had pricked me with a pin," the narrator concludes, "as I was going out, I should have punctured, letting out a loud bawl of laughter which I could hardly keep back in my stomach."[20]

In the introduction to the anthology in which this story also appears, Mphahlele and his co-compiler named American Negro literature, Dickens, and the Russians as giving their cue to South African black literature. Of all Mphahlele's writing this story perhaps comes nearest to Dickensian humor and characterization. All the characters would have sufficient vitality to hold their own in a full-length novel. Like Dickens, Mphahlele is at his best when dealing with the characters of his youth. Also like Dickens, he draws on autobiography when it suits his purpose. The uncle, though not of the stature of a Dickens comic character, is drawn with vigor, consistency, and conviction. There is his unbounded optimism. When he hears that his bribery of the judges was in vain, his immediate fury — "He kept saying, Stupid! Hoodlums! Cheats! Burn the bloody *Afric'* " (the name of the magazine sponsoring the contest) — does not last. "Anyway, neph'," Uncle says, his face cheering up, "two thousand people looking with two eyes each must be better than three men looking with two eyes each, with the possibility of a squint in one of them."[21] When Mary Jane fails to win the beauty contest he rallies quickly once more.

He is a complicated character who faces adversity with dry humor, but this is a protective veneer. Sometimes his sensitivity shows. He laughs at his second wife's bullying and nagging, but he always speaks of her with a sense of hurt. Not, the nephew explains, "such as. a henpecked husband displays. Uncle has tremendous inner resources and plenty of diversions and could not buckle up under his wife's policy of non-collaboration, the way a henpecked man would do."[22]

Although "Grieg on a Stolen Piano," after the novella-length "Mrs. Plum," is the longest story in the collection, there is nothing extraneous to the serious theme of black intellectual struggle in the South African setting. It is a telling condemnation of a society in which a black man of intellect and integrity must founder. Scenes of black-white violent encounter are described realistically, and yet this is not a protest story in the same sense as "We'll Have Dinner at Eight." The protest in "Grieg" arises out of the action of the story.

Here is an economy of words which one does not always find in Mphahlele's writing. In one sentence he describes how the black man sees the white man in the cities: "There was the brief time in 'the kitchens,' as houses of white people are called where one does domestic work, as if the white suburbs were simply a collection of kitchens."[23] The dialogue is always just right and captures South African speech idiom of both black and white. Even the few white characters speak idiomatically, instead of indulging in the stilted talk of "The Living and Dead." For example: "*Hey! Jy! die pikswart een, die bobbejaan!* — the pitch-black one, the baboon," a gang of white boys shouts, for "Uncle is black as a train engine; so black that his face often gives the illusion of being bluish sometimes."[24]

"Excuse, me," Uncle ventures to the new white clerk in a post office, who is keeping a long black line waiting unnecessarily, and explains that he has to get back to his class. "Look here," the clerk replies aggressively, "I'm not only here to serve kaffirs. I'm here to work!" Uncle merely looks at him steadily and the white man recoils at the sight of his face. Then he recovers and shouts: "What are you? What are you? — just a black kaffir, a kaffir monkey, black as tar. Now any more from you and I'll bloody well refuse to serve the whole bloody lot of you. Teacher — teacher, teacher *te hel!*"[25] Uncle does not let him get away with it. He reports the clerk's behavior to his superiors, and he is removed.

Uncle's shrewish second wife is even more forthright than her husband and even less tactful. She disapproves of her step-daughter's weekly night out. "It's choir practice," Uncle says brusquely, and she replies: "Wai-i-i I know much about choir practices, me. A man's daughter can go to them without stopping and one-two-three the next time you look at her she has a big choir practice in her stomach."[26]

The similes and metaphors Mphahlele uses in this story are refreshingly unusual, doing perhaps what the editors of the anthology call violence to standard English, a practice of which they approve. He speaks of the aunt's antheap appearance, for instance. The imagery is concise and often calls attention to the lighter side of the story. After the aunt has made her outrageous comment on her step-daughter's extramural activities, and made the girl run crying to her bedroom, she continues to sit like an antheap, "her larger body seeming to spread wider and wider like an overgrown pumpkin." Uncle confidentially tells his nephew: "One day I'll get so angry, neph', I'll send her away to her people. And at her station I'll put her on a wheelbarrow like a sack of mealies and wheel her right into her people's house if I've to bind her with a rope."[27]

Neither cynicism nor sentimentality mars this successful sketch of a memorable character, which would easily have lent itself to either. Neither the aunt, depicted in only a few references to her by others, nor the village beauty who strides coolly through the machinations around her is a caricature.

IV "A Point of Identity"

In "A Point of Identity" Mphahlele deals more specifically with the political situation in South Africa. We are introduced to the laws that govern the lives of black people, and how they affect them: the Group Areas Act, which confines black, brown, and white people to certain distinct areas, and the act enforcing identity cards which register the holder's race. Sardonically, the author describes the coldness of law and its remoteness from human feelings. This is how he sees the inception of the Population Register Act:

They had long worried about the prospect of one coffee-coloured race, which would shame what they called "white civilization" and "purity" of their European blood. So, maybe, after a sleepless night, someone at his breakfast, read his morning newspapers in between bites, walked about his suburban garden, told his black "boy" to finish cleaning his car, kissed his wife and children goodbye ("don't expect me for supper, dear"), went to the House of Assembly and began to propel a huge legislative measure through the various formal stages to the President's desk where it would be signed as law.[28]

The methods applied in deciding who is "Native" (today "Bantu") — of pure black African ancestry — and who "Coloured" — of mixed blood — would be ridiculous if they were not so tragic in their consequences. Mphahlele changes from a satiric note to one of quiet indignation:

They were ordered to produce evidence to prove their ancestry (was there a white man or woman in the family tree or not?). The onus was clearly on the subject of the inquiry to prove that he was coloured. Day after day papers were filed: birth certificates; photographs; men, women and children came and lined up before this board. A comb was put in their hair; if it fell off, they must have straight or curly hair and so one condition was fulfilled.

"How tall was your father?" a board member might ask. "This high," an exhibit might reply. If he indicated the height by stretching out his arm in a horizontal direction it was likely that the exhibit was Coloured; for Negroes generally indicate height by bending the arm at the elbow so that the forearm points in a vertical direction. . . .

A family woke up one morning wondering if they had been through a dream: some of its members had been declared "Coloured" and others "Native." But how was it possible that a whole family could experience the same dream? Once a "Native," one had to carry a pass to permit him to live in an area, to enter another, to look for work in a town. It would be an indefensible criminal offence if one failed to show the pass to a policeman. Once a "Native," one's wages had to be lowered.[29]

Karel Almeida, the central figure of "A Point of Identity," is a man of light complexion, with a Portuguese surname and an Afrikaans given name, married to a wholly black woman. He has been living in Corner B, a black township outside Pretoria, for many years. When the new law is introduced, Karel succumbs to the temptation of having himself declared colored, and thus gains all the privileges that go with it. He recites the disadvantages of being black to the narrator, a neighboring schoolteacher, who knows them only too well: automatic arrest for not carrying a pass, the hijacking to forced labor farms, lower wages. The narrator, however, is astounded by this betrayal. "But you *are* Negro, Karel. You as good as said so yourself often. You came to live with us blacks because you felt purity of blood was just lunatic nonsense, didn't you?"[30] Karel replies that it is merely the political concept he wishes to discard. He obtains the coveted colored identity card.

Legally, under the Mixed Marriages Act and the Group Areas Act, Karel must now leave the district and abandon his wife, but he makes no attempt to do so. In the meanwhile his leg has begun to trouble him and he has visited a hospital for treatment several times without showing any improvement. Ironically, his "native" wife is prepared to take him to another hospital, if necessary spend all her savings to pay white doctors, while Karel insists on going to a witchdoctor. Karel does not recover. After his death his widow shows the narrator a letter in which the white superintendent of the location asks Karel to leave House No. 35, Mathole Street, and forbids him to occupy another house in the "Bantu location," since he was registered as "Coloured."

Mphahlele takes us back to Second Avenue in this story, but he sees it with a different eye. Karel may be a man whose "whole physical being seemed to be made of laughter," but we only have the narrator's word for it. Karel is not funny in any way, neither in his talk nor in his actions. He has none of the vitality of the earlier township characters. He lacks, in fact, any kind of personality at all. Since the story concerns only his racial dilemma and ends with his death as a solution, it never rises above the political level. Mphahlele is justifiably bitter about South African laws and he is articulate in his protest, but he uses neither invention nor imagery to turn the narrative into imaginative fiction. It is a stirring record of injustice, but so are the many newspaper reports of similar cases, some even more tragic. The narrator's comments read like editorials.

V *"In Corner B"*

By contrast Talita, in the title story, is alive, and the background of township life is woven into the story as an integral part of it. Whereas Karel Almeida is described for the reader, the characters in "In Corner B" and their background come to life through their actions.

Mphahlele goes straight into the story. We hear of a murder as the victim's widow thinks it must have happened. "How can boys just stick a knife into someone's man like that?" Talita muses, while she is waiting for the body to arrive from the mortuary. "Leap out of the dark and start beating up a man and then drive a knife into him." Her sorrow is emphasized and her nature established for the reader instantly when she spares a thought for the parents of the perpetrators even in her own sorrow. "What do the parents of such boys think of them?" she says. "What does it matter now? I'm sitting in this room weeping till my heart wants to break."[31]

The description of the funeral preparations and wake is perhaps Mphahlele's most successful scene of township life. He is now completely confident in expressing himself. The story appeared in *The Classic* in 1964 and must have been written at that time since it would certainly have been published elsewhere first if written earlier. By 1964 *Down Second Avenue* was about to go into a second edition; *African Image* had appeared; Mphahlele had lived in Nigeria, France, and Kenya. He was an established writer and a figure of consequence in the African literary world.

Mphahlele does not use the convention of a narrator in this story, but comments freely as the author upon his characters and their

lives. His "asides" from the dramatic action are full of affectionate
humor about the people among whom he used to live. The customs
connected with death are treated with sympathetic forbearance:
"There are a number of things city folk can afford to do
precipitately; a couple may marry by special licence and listen to
enquiries from their next-of-kin after the fact; they can be
precipitate in making children and marry after the event; children
will break with their parents and lose themselves in other townships; several parents do not hold coming-out parties to celebrate the
last day of a new-born baby's month-long confinement in the house.
But death humbles the most unconventional, the hardest rebel. The
dead person cannot simply be packed off to the cemetery."[32]

Even death is an occasion here for living fully. We see the people
at the wake eating, drinking, and laughing. Relatives and friends
"and their relatives and *their* friends" come from afar. There is
"singing, praying, singing, preaching,"[33] women screaming in high-
pitched voices, political discussions with acid comments that if a
white man had been the victim, the murderers would already have
been caught. Women serve tea and sandwiches. Cousin Stoffel is the
self-appointed and not altogether trusted collector of contributions
for funeral expenses, which he enters in a school exercise book. The
money helps to buy liquor from a shebeen.

Talita sleeps where she sits and is disturbed only to be asked
questions occasionally, like "What will you eat now?" or "Has your
headache stopped today?" or "Are your bowels moving properly?"
or "The burial society wants your marriage certificate, where do you
keep it?"[34]

The plot of the story concerns the love between Talita and her
husband. It is a simple and unembellished love story, tender without
sentimentality. Talita, a lively and over-talkative, but affectionate
woman, loves her gentle shy man. We see "her man" through her
eyes: he was, as she remembers now after his death, "tall, not very
handsome but lovable; an insurance agent who moved about in a
car." He was therefore more successful than most, since others in the
business usually walked from house to house and used buses and
trains between townships. Her man "had soft gentle eyes and was
not at all as vivacious as she."[35]

They had been married for nineteen years and had three children
when something occurred which darkened the brightness of their intense love for each other. A love letter from a woman to her husband
fell into Talita's hands. As in her thoughts immediately after his
death, Talita's thoughts turned from the center of the drama. She

wondered how a mistress should come to entrust a confidential letter
to a messenger stupid enough not to return it if the man should be
out.

Talita remembers the incident now, as she sits at the wake. Her
thoughts are like disjointed lines running around in circles, but
always she tries to keep the image of her man before her. In his gentle manner he had confessed his faithlessness. He had promised not
to see the other woman again and they continued as before. Soon,
however, Talita had noticed that the mistress was still in the picture
and she tracked her down. "No one was going to share her man with
her, fullstop,"[36] she said to herself in her forthright way. She walked
in on the unsuspecting mistress. Her words to the woman's husband
were outspoken. " 'I am glad you are in, *Morena* — sir. I have just
come to ask you to chain your bitch. That is my man and mine
alone.' She stood up to leave."[37]

We now have one of Mphahlele's few sexual scenes, handled with
great delicacy, between the shy husband and the woman who often
blusters but is at heart as soft and timid as he is. Sex to Mphahlele is
synonymous with love. The intensity of the scene makes it far more
personal than anything Mphahlele has written about the women in
his own life. This, one feels, is Mphahlele's idea of ideal love.

Often there were moments of deep silence as Talita and her man sat
together or lay side by side. But he seldom stiffened up. He would take her
into his arms and love her furiously and she would respond generously and
tenderly because she loved him and the pathos in his eyes.
"You know, my man," she ventured to say one evening in bed, "if there is
anything I can help you with, if there is anything you would like to tell me,
you mustn't be afraid to tell me. There may be certain things a woman can
do for her man which he never suspected she could do."
"Oh, don't worry about me. There is nothing you need do for me." And,
like someone who had at last found a refuge after a rough and dangerous
journey, her man would fold her in his arms and love her.[38]

Mphahlele completes his picture of a woman in love. "Funny,"
Talita, who is completely articulate, wonders to herself, "that you
saw your man's face every day almost and yet you couldn't look at it
while he slept without the sensation of some guilt or something timid
or tense or something held in suspension; so that if the man stirred,
your heart gave a leap as you turned your face away. One thing she
was sure of amidst all the wild and agonizing speculation: her man
loved her and their children."[39]

Mphahlele has learnt the effect of and necessity for comic relief

after a tense and dramatic scene. He thus switches back to the wake
and we have the relatives quarrelling over precedence. One out-
raged cousin begins a long harangue but is rebuked by "uncle of the
clan," who says that she has not got "what the English call respec-
tion." In another corner an elderly relative serves drinks to " 'drown
de sorry, as the Englishman says.' "[40]

The alternation between scenes of the quiet and tender past and
the noisy present provides a most effective contrast. Equally successful is the contrast between the reality of death and the humor of
a scene in which a black constable drags in two disreputable young
suspects in handcuffs for Talita to identify. He abuses and swears at
them, but he beats a hasty retreat when one of the older women
relatives brandishes a stick at him and admonishes him for distur-
bing the peace of the widow and for using foul language. Repeating
some of his own words, she says to him: "Go and tell that government of yours that he is full of dung to send you to do such thing.
Sies! Kgoboromente kgoboromente! You and him can go to hell
where you belong. Get out!"[41]

Finally the two themes of past and present, of drama and humor,
are brought together in a highly climactic funeral scene. Marta, the
mistress, appears at the cemetery seemingly out of nowhere, and
flings herself on the grave. Talita is badly shaken, but she is led away
to the car before she can act.

In his earlier fiction Mphahlele might have left the story on this
note. Here, however, he provides us with relief from tension and at
the same time with a perfect and touching ending to the love story
between Talita and her husband. Out of his grave he declares his
love for her, and he does so, gently as in his life time, through the
barely literate medium of his mistress, Marta. Talita receives a letter
from Marta which is well worth quoting in full:

Dear Missis Molamo, I am dropping this few lines for to hoping that you are
living good now i want to teling you my hart is sore sore i hold myselfe bad
on the day of youre mans funeral my hart was ful of pane too much i see
myselfe already o Missis Molamo alreaddy doing mad doings i think the
gods are beatting me now for holding myselfe as wyle animall forgeef
forgeef i pray with all my hart child of the people.[42]

Talita, flushing with anger, wonders whether she should continue to
read. "These wild women," she says to herself, "who can't even
write must needs try to do so in English." But she continues.

now i must tel you something you must noe quik quik thees that i can see that when you come to my hause and then whenn you see me kriing neer the grafe i can see you think i am sweet chokolet of your man i can see you think in your hart my man love that wooman no no i want to tel you that he neva love me nevaneva he livd same haus my femily rented in Fitas and i lovd him mad i tel you i lovd him mad i wanted him with red eyes he was nise leetl bit nise to me but i see he sham for me as i have got no big ejucashin he got too much book i make nise tea and cake for him and he like my muther and he is so nise i want to foss him to love me but he just nise i am shoor he come to meet me in toun even now we are 2 merryd peeple bicos he remember me and muther looked aftar him like bruther for me he was stil nise to me but al wooman can see whenn there is no loveness in a man and they can see lovfulness. now he is gonn i feel i want to rite with my al ten fingas becos i have too muche to say aboute your sorriness and my sorriness i will help you to kry you help me to kry and leev that man in peas with his gods. so i stop press here my deer i beg to pen off the gods look aftar us

i remain your sinserity
Missis Marta Shuping.[43]

How does Talita react to this revelation? She stands up and makes tea for herself. Her love has been restored to her. She feels "like a foot traveller after a good refreshing bath."[44]

The more one reads Mphahlele's stories of township life, the greater becomes one's understanding of the term "acceptance" he uses to describe a phase in his fiction. This is not acceptance of township conditions or of life in South Africa; rather acceptance of the fact that human values of love, trust, and loyalty can continue even under impossible living conditions. In this story he calls it "surrender" rather than acceptance, a poetic surrender to life and death, underlying which is "the one long and huge irony of endurance."[45]

The background is never allowed to obtrude for its own sake. At this time African writing was becoming popular with European readers, and many writers deliberately emphasized the un-European aspect of African life by giving lengthy anthropological explanations. With Mphahlele, on the other hand, African customs become an essential part of the story. Talita can lie back and indulge in her bittersweet memories because she knows that tradition and custom will take care of everything necessary for the wake and funeral. Interspersed with her thoughts are the inevitable acts and movements leading steadily toward the last rites for the dead. The story is

static neither in the present nor in the past but leads toward their
meeting place in organized rhythm.

VI "Mrs. Plum"

Another well-organized story is the novella, "Mrs. Plum." This is
Mphahlele's most serious attempt to explore the relationship between white and black in South Africa. Once again two protagonists
face each other.

Mrs. Plum, a widow living in the white suburb of Greenside with
her daughter Kate, her servants and her dogs, is concerned about the
welfare of Africans. She goes to meetings with others who think like
her. They work toward including a few black people in the government of the country, electing their own representative to rule the
tribal villages, and obtaining higher wages and generally better
treatment. She writes newspaper articles and she joins the protest
meetings of the Black Sash, an organization of women who protest
by standing silently in front of parliament and government offices,
wearing a black sash of mourning across their shoulders. She runs
night classes for servants to teach them to read and write, and she
helps her own servant with her English. Her servant is asked to sit at
the table at meals.

All this we learn from the servant, Karabo, who is the narrator.
Karabo is, or pretends to be, an ingenue who asks Mrs. Plum's
daughter Kate all the wrong questions. "My mother," says Kate,
"goes to meetings many times." Karabo asks "What for?"; and in
response to Kate's reply, "For your people," she says: "My people
are in Phokeng far away. They have got mouths. . . . Why does she
want to say something for them?" Kate explains patiently that she
means all the black people in the country. "Oh," says Karabo in-
nocently, "What do the black people want to say?"[16]

The subtle irony, which raises this story, like "Grieg on a Stolen
Piano" above the mere protest level, is conveyed in the following
dialogue between the two girls. Kate is telling Karabo about the
protest meetings of the Black Sash organization.

My mother and the others go and stand where the people in government are
going to enter or go out of a building.
I ask her I say, Does the government and the white people listen and stop
their sins? She says. No. But my mother is in another group of white people.
I ask, Do the people of the government give the women tea and cakes?
Kate says, Karabo! How stupid; oh!
I say to her I say, Among my people if someone comes and stands in front

of my house I tell him to come in and I give him food. You white people are wonderful. But they keep standing there and the government people do not give them anything.

She replies, You mean strange. How many times have I taught you not to say *wonderful* when you mean *strange!* Well, Kate says with a short heart and looking cross and she shouts, Well they do not stand there the whole day to ask for tea and cakes stupid. Oh dear![47]

Karabo dislikes eating at the table because she is not used to eating with a knife and fork, because she prefers the kind of food she eats at home and which other servants may cook for themselves, but mainly because it frightens her. Working for Mrs. Plum is agreeable, however, for she is paid regularly and not abused as in her previous two positions, and many of her friends are working near her. And her employer does teach her to cook and to follow recipes, and praises her when she does well.

Mrs. Plum's liberalism Karabo finds puzzling but accepts at first as one of the eccentricities of the white race. This one, "my madam . . . loved dogs and Africans and said that everyone must follow the law even if it hurt. These were three big things in Madam's life."[48] Thus the story opens. It ends when Mrs. Plum visits Karabo in her home village, after she has left her job, and begs her to return. She tells Karabo that her two pet dogs have died. Did this woman, Karabo wonders, come to ask her to return because she has lost two animals she loved? Mrs. Plum says to her, "You know, I like your people, Karabo, the Africans." "And Dick and me?" Karabo wonders.[49] In between we gradually realize that while Mrs. Plum's liberalism is quite genuine, unlike that of Miss Pringle, it is completely impersonal, directed at ideas rather than at people. Mphahlele dislikes this type so intensely because it lacks the one characteristic that is his own ruling passion: a feeling of compassion for one's fellowmen.

Karabo joins a sewing circle where she learns to understand politics as well as sewing. Here she learns the rules of domestic service: that while there are good madams and masters and bad ones, a master and a servant can never be friends. Even the good ones are subject to the ABC of black-white relationship:

You are not even sure if the ones you say are good are not like that because they cannot breathe or live without the work of your hands. As long as you need their money, face them with respect. But you must know that many sad things are happening in our country and you, all of you, must always be learning, adding to what you already know, and obey us when we ask you to help us.[50]

We follow Karabo in her life at work as a domestic servant and in her leisure hours. She is a happy and intelligent girl who takes note of all that goes on around her. When she entered Mrs. Plum's employ, she had not been away from her home village for long. She is still feeling her way, gauging how far one can go with one's employer.

Karabo finds Madam more and more difficult to understand. "Every time I thought of Madam, she became more and more like a dark forest which one learns to enter, and which one will never know. But there were several times when I thought, this woman is easy to understand, she is like all other white women."[51] Thus, Mrs. Plum and Karabo unwittingly share one attitude toward each other. To Mrs. Plum, Karabo is an African, an inferior creature who must be treated with kindness; to Karabo, Mrs. Plum is a madam to whom one adjusts as one of the necessities of life. It never occurs to either to think of the other as a person with an individuality.

The contrast between black and white, and the progress of the story, are recorded by the sound of laughter, the timbre changing according to the situation. Karabo is full of laughter because she is young, and, though life is hard, it is full of fun and promise. She shares her laughter with her friends, Chimane who works next door and introduced her to the job, and Dick, the young man who works in the garden and looks after Mrs. Plum's dogs. They laugh for the joy of living, and this is something that is lacking in the life of the white suburban housewife. It makes Mrs. Plum uneasy. Sometimes the laughter becomes a little harsher. One needs a sense of humor as a servant. Dick, who nearly rolls on the ground laughing at funny incidents and imitates Mrs. Plum drinking tea to perfection, is afraid of white people and terrified of the police.

The laughter in the house soon ceases altogether. Karabo becomes more and more uneasy. Mrs. Plum has been giving a number of parties. Karabo does not like the Africans who are invited, who treat her as an inferior and make her feel ashamed. The only exceptions are a black doctor and his sister, who come to the kitchen to chat with her. Then Kate, who is of the same age as Karabo, and with whom she has contact on a more personal footing than with her mistress, announces that she is in love with the black doctor. They will leave the country and marry elsewhere.

Both Mrs. Plum and Karabo are horrified. Mrs. Plum has not expected her daughter to take her ideas literally, and Karabo feels
betrayed, not so much because she herself is in love with the doctor
— she knows that he is beyond her reach even if he has been kind to
her — but because Kate now appears to her as a thief, a "fox that
falls upon a flock of sheep at night."[52] There is silence in the house;
the laughter and joy have fled. Karabo sends her current boyfriend
away. She cannot sleep at night and when she does, her dreams are
"full of painful things."[53]

Kate confronts Karabo. She wants to know why Karabo does not
like the idea of marriage between white and black. Karabo cannot
answer. She feels confused. "All I could say was I said to your
mother I had never seen a black man and a white woman marrying,
you hear me? What I think about it is my business."[54]

Winter comes. White suburbia empties, as families and their nan-
nies seek warmer climes at the seaside, leaving the other servants
behind to mind the house and the pets. Joy is revived for a while, but
the laughter is still uneasy. The servants hold a party in one of the
houses, where they dance and sing and eat, not in the servants'
quarters, but inside the house. The risk doubtless adds to the fun.

There is no trouble, but no sooner is Mrs. Plum back from her
holiday when trouble begins. Police come to look for black people
not entitled to be in the neighborhood, and now we have yet another
kind of laughter. Mrs. Plum and Karabo get together for once and
join forces against the intruders. The police have asked to search her
house and Mrs. Plum refuses. They force their way to the back. Mrs.
Plum turns the garden hose on them, and Karabo switches on the
tap. The next day Mrs. Plum is arrested for obstructing the police.
She refuses to pay her fine and goes to jail for fourteen days.

Karabo is impressed. She acknowledges that Mrs. Plum is genuine
in her convictions. Did not the sewing teacher say "You must be
ready to go to jail for the things you believe are true and for which
you are taken by the police?"[55] Karabo says to herself: "This woman,
hai, I do not know she seems to think very much of us black
people."[56] After this Kate comes home again and acquires a white
boyfriend. Karabo too meets a new boy with whom she falls in love.
She and Kate are friends again.

But once again the laughter vanishes. Karabo's news of home is
only of friends who have died. Here, in the suburbs, there is also un-
happiness. Chimane is pregnant. Her boyfriend is willing to marry
her, but the tragedy is an economic one. "*Hai*, Karabo . . . Do you

not see that I have not worked long enough for my people? If I marry now who will look after them when I am the only child?" Money is the main concern and a problem always just under the surface. "The light goes out in my mind," says Karabo, "and I cannot think of the right answer. How many times have I feared the same thing! Luck and the mercy of the gods that is all I live by. That is all we live by — all of us."[57] This reminds Karabo that there is another life, a real life, among her own people, and she is suddenly sickened by the smell of the cosmetics she shares with Mrs. Plum, by the dogs, by Dick cleaning out the dirt of Madam's body from the bath.

The story continues on a darker note. Chimane has an abortion in the township of Alexandria, "that terrible township where night and day are full of knives and bicycle chains and guns and the barking of hungry dogs and of people in trouble."[58] Dick is worried about his job because he is heavily in debt through his efforts to keep his sister at school. Then a rumor starts that Johannesburg servants are going to poison the dogs of the white people. The police come to investigate. Mrs. Plum no longer trusts Dick. She asks Karabo whether Dick is trustworthy. "She asked me she said Karabo, do you think Dick is a boy we can trust?"[59] Karabo does not know what to answer, since she cannot accept the "we," but eventually she comforts Mrs. Plum against her will. "Dick is all right, madam, I found myself saying."[60] Although Dick would not dream of poisoning the dogs, the police come again and again, and eventually Mrs. Plum dismisses him. This, as we know, is a catastrophe for him.

Relations between Mrs. Plum and Karabo now break down altogether. Karabo is hurt and angry about Dick's dismissal. Karabo receives more news of death from her home town, including that of her mother's brother, a relationship considered closer by Africans than that of any other uncle. Karabo wants to go home, and when Mrs. Plum will give her only leave without pay, she tells her that she is leaving for good. Her reference says only that Karabo worked for Mrs. Plum for three years.

Karabo is glad to be home, but she knows she will return to Johannesburg eventually. Then one day a red car arrives in the village and in it is Mrs. Plum come to ask her to work for her again. Karabo boldly states her terms, an increase in wages and in the amount of leave, and Mrs. Plum accepts. Karabo now feels surer of herself, since she has won this round, and Mrs. Plum seems kinder. But when Karabo hears that the dogs Monty and Malan are dead, she suspects Mrs. Plum's kindness. Did she like Africans in the same

way as she liked dogs? People, after all, are individuals. Thus Karabo
wonders, and Dick and herself, did she like them?

The story is a tragic one because of its inner and factual truth. It is
the tragedy of South Africa. Here are two people, each representing
her race in some of its better qualities, who genuinely try to understand each other, and fail miserably. Mrs. Plum thinks she likes
Karabo and makes an effort to be a just employer; Karabo can sympathize with her employer. "There was something in Mrs. Plum's
face as she was speaking which made me fear her and pity her at the
same time . . . there was something on that face that told me she
wanted me on her side," she says, when Mrs. Plum asks her whether
Dick is trustworthy. But gradually Karabo realizes that there can be
no friendship between white employer and black employee. Life can
become tolerable only if the relationship is based on dissembling.
They must feel around each other, each finding out how far she can
go. It is in their lies that they understand each other. When Mrs.
Plum returns from jail she says that life has been good there. Yet
Karabo understands that she is ashamed of having been there, not,
she says "like our black people who are always being put in jail and
only look at it as the white man's evil game." It was easy for Karabo
to lie to a white madam. When Chimane went to have an abortion
Karabo tells her "white people" that she was ill and had been
fetched to her village by a brother. "They would never try to find
out. They seldom did, these people. Give them any lie, and it will do.
For they seldom believe you whatever you say. And how can a black
person work for white people and be afraid to tell them lies. They are
always asking the questions, you are always the one to give the
answers."[61]

Thus Karabo finds a *modus vivendi.* When Mrs. Plum comes to
visit her in her home village, however, it is a different matter. How
little they have thought about each other as people is emphasized by
Karabo's predicament. She tells us:

I did not know what to do and how to look at her as she spoke to me. So I
looked at the piece of cloth I was sewing pictures on. There was a tired but
soft smile on her face. Then I remembered that she might want to sit. I went
inside to fetch a low bench for her. When I remembered it afterwards, the
thought came to me that there are things I never think white people can
want to do at our homes when they visit for the first time: like sitting, drinking water or entering the house.[62]

The gulf is obviously so wide that it can never be bridged. Never. There is no hope.

The characters tune in with the theme fairly well, although their roles are the most important thing about them. Karabo is completely believable. She is honest and sincere toward her friends, aware of her responsibility toward her parents. She is bright, intelligent, and cheerful, always ready to laugh, but aware of the serious side of life. She knows her limitations; for instance, that the black doctor, "so full of knowledge and English,"[63] is beyond her reach.

As a narrator she is perfect. The story never wavers, as Karabo tells it in her forthright way. She never falls out of character. Her thought processes are uncomplicated, but her grasp of a situation always shrewd. For instance, when she leaves Mrs. Plum, she knows she is going to return to Johannesburg. "Money was little, but life was full and it was better than sitting in Phokeng and watching the sun rise and set."[64]

It is understood that Karabo is telling the story to a friend, and she would thus be talking in her own language. Mphahlele indicates this subtly without resorting to tricks. There is an undefinable African intonation in the narrative, a smooth rhythm achieved without the mock-Biblical language and repetition of phrases to which Alan Paton resorts in *Cry, the Beloved Country*. Mphahlele also makes use of quaint and attractive phrases. "I held my heart in my hands," says Karabo when she visits Chimane after her abortion. Chimane's aunt, who says she would have looked after the child, chides Chimane for getting rid of it. "She has allowed a worm to cut the roots, I don't know."[65]

Mrs. Plum is considerably less believable. Mphahlele's dislike of this type of liberal has already been referred to. She scores over previous white stock characters in Mphahlele's fiction in that she does have several facets to her nature, but when they are put together they still fail to make up a person we have met and known. We are told, for instance, that her husband committed suicide. She is the title character of a long story, yet we are not told why he did so nor anything at all about their relationship. The fact that she has sexual relations with her pet dogs is completely out of character and has only symbolic meaning, as we shall see.

Her attitude toward her daughter, however, is a perfectly normal one. Kate is a modern miss, wild and headstrong, who fights with her mother, makes a bid for independence by threatening to marry a black man, and then settles down to white middle-class existence.

She is introduced mainly as a contrast in her relationship with Karabo. They are both twenty-two and enjoy a superficial form of friendship. Kate meets Karabo on her own terms. She has not yet become an employer, one of "them," but given time she doubtless will.

The minor characters are well drawn. Dick is a very young man, who combines boyish fun, serious ambitions, and a tender love for his sister with terror of white authority. He provides most of the humor in the story. We can almost hear the laughter as he imitates Mrs. Plum. He swears that one day white people will put earrings and toe-rings and bangles on their dogs. That would be the day he would leave Mrs. Plum, he says, for he was sure that she would want him to polish the rings and bangles with Brasso.

Dick is compassionate. He disapproves of poisoning the white people's dogs, even if they give him so much work. "Dick kept saying It is wrong this thing they want to do to kill poor dogs. What have these things of God done to be killed for? Is it the dogs that make us carry passes? Is it dogs that make the laws that give us pain? People are just mad, they do not know what they want, stupid!"[66] But his laughter and compassion turn to bitterness when he is unjustly dismissed. He would still not poison the dogs, he says, but "I do not care what happens to the dumb things, now."[67] At the end the dogs are stolen, Mrs. Plum tells Karabo, and probably dead. For a moment Karabo wonders, "I thought of Dick . . . could he?"[68] But it seems unlikely.

As in previous stories, animals are used as symbols, and here very successfully. Malan and Monty — felicitous choice of names — the one with long hair and small black eyes "and a face nearly like that of an old woman,"[69] the other bigger and short-haired — are of no named breed, but we see them shuffling and grunting their way through the story. Basically, they stand for white suburbia and its pretensions. In Mrs. Plum's life they represent her forced love for inferior creatures, be they human or animal. To the servants they stand for everything unpleasant in their work and in their relationship with their employers. It is beyond Dick's comprehension that anyone should talk to dogs. It is because of the dogs that he loses his job and will probably be unable to give his clever little sister an education. Chimane has to get rid of her baby because she cannot afford to stop work, but the white people are planning to buy land for a cemetery for dogs. Friends of Karabo's once dug up a dead dog buried between sheets. They kept the sheets and threw the dog in a lake.

This is closer to the bone and more realistic in its meaning than Evelyn Waugh's satire in *The Loved One*, which possibly gave Mphahlele some of the ideas used in this story.

Karabo at first accepts the dogs as one of Madam's eccentricities, though they make her "fed up." As her relationship with Mrs. Plum deteriorates, so does her attitude toward the dogs. When Malan sniffs at her legs she put her foot "under its fat belly and shoved it up and away . . . so that it cried *tjunk - tjunk - tjunk* as it went out. . . . I say to it," she reports, "I say Go and tell your brother what I have done to you and tell him to try it and see what I will do. Tell your grandmother when she comes home too."[70]

Mrs. Plum's sexual acts with the dogs, which Dick and Karabo watch through a keyhole, symbolizes Mrs. Plum's neurotic, sterile existence, as contrasted with Chimane whom circumstances force to get rid of her child. In the end the dogs become part of Karabo's dream as she sits nodding in the bus which is taking her to her village. In her dream Dick kills the dogs and Mrs. Plum buries them in clean pink sheets, but they insist on coming out of their hole. She wakes up in a sweat. Finally, as we have seen, they symbolize Mrs. Plum's attitude toward Africans. Mphahlele describes "Mrs. Plum" still today as "the best thing I ever pulled off."[71] It was chosen by Charles Larson for his anthology, *African Short Stories*.

CHAPTER 6

Essays and Critical Works

THE story of Mphahlele's life after leaving South Africa
is one of ideas rather than events. Whatever literary, cultural,
social, and political problems involved Africans, interested and involved him. In his search for place and self-identification, and for
the direction which the African as a black man in general and the
black writer in particular must follow, Mphahlele investigated and
interpreted current ideas such as protest in literature, negritude, the
black aesthetic. He lectured, attended congresses, and wrote essays
on these subjects. He published two book-length works, *The African
Image* (1962; new and revised edition, 1973) and *Voices in the
Whirlwind and Other Essays* (1972). He has asked specifically to
have his ideas judged according to the second version of *The African
Image* and *Voices in the Whirlwind*, indicating that he has repudi-
ated those sections in the earlier version of *Image* that he has altered.
It is interesting, however, to study both versions together, in order to
follow the development of his ideas.

I The African Image

This work has as its nucleus a still earlier work, Mphahlele's
Master of Arts thesis written in 1956. It also incorporates other
writing, such as an essay entitled "Black and White" which Mphahlele wrote for the *New Statesman* in 1960. The resulting variety of
subject matter and style, as well as the many attempts at defining
and redefining and at classification, detract from the unity and
coherence of the work. In this respect the new version is possibly
more confusing than the earlier one.

Mphahlele himself sees *The African Image* as an examination of
attitudes toward color, and it is evident that he regards this theme as
sufficiently strong to hold the work together. From there he felt he
could go on to talk about whatever interested him and (in his judg-

ment) his readers. In spite of frequent definitions and of his avowed aim to seek definition of both self and Africa, he emphasizes fluidity and lack of permanence, the overlapping of images, and the blurring of categories. This he makes clear in the title quotations from Marcus Aurelius and Emerson, respectively.

Soon will the earth cover us all: then the earth, too, will change, and the things also which result from the change will continue to change forever, and these again forever. For if man reflects on the changes and transformations which follow one another like wave after wave and their rapidity, he will despise everything which is perishable.

There are no fixtures in nature. The universe is fluid and volatile. Permanence is but a word of degrees.[1]

Mphahlele stresses this aspect of the fluid and the transitory, especially in the new version, by presenting his thoughts as musings. This he does by means of half-sentences, incomplete statements, and phrases thrown out to the reader. The accent is always on seeking, not on finding the answer. He does not hesitate to change his mind or to explore new directions. Thus *African Image* should be regarded as an indication of black thought and its relationship to various geographical, historical, racial, and cultural factors, as seen by one intelligent, well-read, and well-travelled man, who does not pretend to be objective. Only in this way can we appreciate much of what Mphahlele wants to tell us.

Why does Mphahlele find it necessary to explore the African image, and just what does he mean by it? When visiting Britain and the United States for the first time, he recalls (in the introduction to the first edition of *The African Image*) he was constantly required to "put [himself] across" — in other words, to explain himself as a black man to the white man. This is what he "choose[s] to call the African Image."[2] He explains that he often found it necessary to change his stance and overhaul his attitudes. "My purpose," he says in the preface to the first edition, "in raising it all in this book is as much to try to evaluate the sense and nonsense that is often said and thought by whites and blacks, top dogs and underdogs about each other and about themselves."[3] There can be no total image, he warns us. With a vibrant people, whatever single image may emerge must shift.

Mphahlele's emphasis is always on the black man in a contemporary and geographic context. The African personality must be explored, even if it hurts, "without flinching at the social realities of our time,"[4] he tells black writers. In 1958, when Kwame Nkrumah gave voice to the concept of the "African Personality" at the All-African People's Conference held in Accra, it meant one thing. Only four independent African countries were represented then, the rest of the conference being made up of nationalist movements. "The personality that Nkrumah talked about was a beacon on the battlefield, a thrust, an assertion of the African's presence; it was a coming into consciousness of the African," Mphahlele says.[5] Today, with most of Africa independent, the concept means something different. In the former French colonies, where the colonial power treated its subjects as black Frenchmen and the black man aspired to be black and different, it is one thing; in South Africa, where the oppressor makes the difference paramount and the black man aspires to be equal, it is another. In the diaspora the black man has yet another personality. Is there, then, a common bond in being black which can be described as the African personality? Mphahlele quotes the West Indian poet Aimé Cesaire, when he says *chacun à sa negritude propre.* Mphahlele's own African-ness tells him to turn away from the Christian-Hebraic god, and the Islamic god, toward his own ancestors, forces that are closer to him. "We have each his own *chi.*"[6] This aspect, and an African direction and relevance in cultural education, he sees as the essentials. Others, he allows, stress other aspects: "Each to his own."[7]

It is for these reasons of diversity in definition and interpretation that Mphahlele opposes the concept of negritude, a term coined by Cesaire to create pride in the Negro in his blackness, based on pride in his history, philosophy, and culture before the advent of the white man. Mphahlele feels that negritude fails to give voice to African meaning in the present living context. He does not reject the historical relevance of negritude, but says that the historical factors that gave rise to it have ceased to exist. He finds the preoccupation with anthropology of its exponents irrelevant for the black man of today in South Africa, for instance, who lives in a multiracial society. Black Frenchmen may have to remind themselves that they are black, but no black South African is ever allowed to forget it. "If there is any *negritude* in the black man's art in South Africa," he says, "it is because we *are* African. If a writer's tone is healthy he is bound to express the African in him."[8] He thus echoes Wole Soyinka's famous saying that a black man no more has to proclaim his negritude than a tiger his tigritude. To realists like Soyinka and

Mphahlele, negritude is a pose, an artifical structure, so much intellectual talk, which interferes with the real business of being a black man and a black writer today. In South Africa the black man is occupied with a very real fight against government efforts to legislate him back to his tribe, to force him to accept the fabricated concept of "Bantu culture." "We daren't look back," Mphahlele says.[9]

In the revised edition of *African Image* Mphahlele heads the chapter on this theme "Negritude revisited." He is no more enchanted with the concept than he was during his first encounter. Only the educated African from abroad can afford to walk about "with his mouth open, startled by the beauty of African women, by the black man's 'heightened sensitivity.'" "It is all so embarrassing," Mphahlele comments.[10] Then there are the "passionate continentals," who are "having a weird affair with franco-phone Africa."[11] Their attitude he rejects as being patronizing and tiresome.

Negritude, Mphahlele tells us, can have meaning only if one regards it as a social force, never static, a tension, a continuing movement that asserts the value of African culture and its institutions of learning. If that is its function, he says, "let it shake its rhetoric-saturated, lyric-larded backside and get to work. If it does not, let it shut up."[12] At any rate, it must climb down from its stale presidential, ambassadorial, conference, festival, elite platform and listen to the real cries of Africa.

Here Mphahlele shows his disillusionment, not with negritude, to which he never subscribed, but with the achievements under its banner for which he had had some hope. He feels that most of the originators did not really understand what they were up against: that the white world might be quite willing to concede the black man his culture and would even ask to be invited to his arts festivals, but would continue to manipulate him politically and economically. Negritude as an artistic program, he insists, has proved itself unworkable for modern Africa. He remains the realist who entreats the exponents of negritude to "stop telling the masses how beautiful they are while they are starving."[13] There is a definite shift in the readership at which he aims, between the old and the new version. In the second edition he seems to be addressing the black Americans among whom he lives rather than the white man to whom he previously felt he had to explain himself.

As far as America is concerned, Mphahlele has little time for the

Afro-American who "almost literally grovels on his stomach so as to rub Africa's earth into his skin as a symbol of edification."[14] The arrogance of the black Americans in choosing a name for the future independent black South Africa, for instance, repels him. He gives a brief survey of survivals of Africa in black America: culture such as spontaneous dancing, folk tales based on African legends, certain rituals in religious worship. He then investigates the role of Africa in black America and tests Afro-American writers like Claude McKay, Countee Cullen, Arna Bontemps, and others against a yardstick of genuine emotional attachment to the continent. They often fail in that they merely strike a posture, climb on the bandwagon, indulge in rhetorical stance, he says. The dream that Africa can serve as a leaven to universal civilization, he feels, has been shattered by events. He comes to the conclusion that black Americans must still get to know Africa as she is, and not as a mere grand idea, if black people of the world are to have something to give one another. At the moment, he says, "we are playing games."[15]

There is little change in his attitude in these matters during the eleven years between publication of the two editions, though his utterances in the later work are based on a wider knowledge of African and Afro-American literature and philosophy. In other spheres, however, his travels and reading have affected his mental development considerably.

The man who rejected his church with great trepidation while in South Africa has become confident in his repudiation of the Christian faith. He now feels an affinity with African religion, which black South African intellectuals still living in an atmosphere of black inferiority at home would find horrifying. His attitude, however, is a practical rather than a religious one. His ancestors, he feels, can help the African "snap out of the trance into which we were thrown by western education." The significance is not that the black man can go back to ancestor worship, but that the ancestors have historical and spiritual relevance, and thus help to free him mentally. Christianity, and also Islam, are not rejected on emotional or even historical grounds but on the political level. It does not involve the black man. "*Why now should we be fed on the history, the folklore, the allegory and poetry of the Hebrews (however beautiful) who had no functional connection with Africa? Why be tied to the shackles of Christ's and Muhammed's ideas when we have our own ancient liberal wisdom?*" he asks, with the emphasis of italics.[16]

In politics his attitude toward South Africa has hardened. There is a definite shift toward revolutionary action. A nonracial South African society is still his ideal, but since the white man "has done everything to drag this idea into the mud,"[17] he no longer feels optimistic about a possibility of achieving it. The emphasis now is on black nationalism as an instrument for freedom and fulfillment. The whites would now have the choice of becoming African or leaving. The aspect of *apartheid,* separate development, by which the black man must abandon the towns and cities for the underdeveloped barren tribal lands, according to an unpopular ethnic grouping, is particularly abhorrent to him.

His political comments raise no new issues. He does not aspire to being a political philosopher; his function is to interpret. Yet he is not always clear in his discussions. A great deal of his comment on South African politics in the new version is incomprehensible to anyone not closely versed in the subject. Expressions like "tribal colleges," for example — university colleges confined by law to students of the particular tribe preponderant in that area — are not explained. Mphahlele expresses anger about splinter groups in the exiled freedom movements, which requires a knowledge of these movements to appreciate. He seems to expect the reader of the new version of *Image* to have read the first edition.

In *The African Image* Mphahlele's anger is more intellectualized and less convincing in its expression than it was in the autobiography *Down Second Avenue,* which was written at a time when he was tasting the bitterness himself. His hatred of whites is no longer a tangible thing, and he is aware of it. "Having been born and raised right in the center of racial conflict," he says, "you could not view your life objectively." Objectivity is a luxury which he still cannot allow himself, but

after you come out of Southern Africa, you realize how much more you hate whites as a group than you did in the rough and tumble of black-white relationships. There is everything human about whites when you are close to them, when they kick you around. I mean you feel them physically, and you see them as human beings. *That* is your reality. Your reaction to their brutality is mostly that of distrust, fear and anger. There is something about the act and fact of communal survival *inside* a situation of racism that either tones down, or lends another complexion to, the hate that is mixed with anger. *Outside* the situation, you are on your own, you have little communal support: at best, it is intellectual. So you hate the whites you left behind with a scalding intensity. Could it be that distance creates a void and that the burning lava of hate *must* fill it?[18]

Mphahlele is thus in the position of the angry young men of England in the 1950's, who also were angry in the abstract rather than personally involved. It did not mean that their feelings were less strong or purposeful.

In many ways *The African Image* is a continuation or, at times, a re-thinking of his autobiography. Actual events are mentioned. He tells of his life in Nigeria and of his first visit to England and his reaction to it of "near neurotic tremor." "The last line of my diary of the visit reads," he tells us, " *'I've tried to read Britain — or what part of it I've seen — letter for letter, like a child learning how to read. Each letter had been a huge impression, and the sum total has left me a bundle of agitation. How long freedom is going to intensify my hatred of those who have denied me it, I don't know.'* "[19]

He recalls his childhood in the rugged mountains of the Northern Transvaal and his mother's ambitions for him, but this time he talks of these matters to a purpose. His mother, and many others like her, wanted their sons to have an education in order to help improve the lot of the black man, economically on the family plane, politically on the community level. But their hopes led to disillusionment.

The dreams about his youth are the longings of the exile. They are guilty dreams; he feels he should be back in Johannesburg. "Teach the youth what the government syllabus says and use it to sow the seeds of rebellion, and set on fire the passions that are already raging, waiting for articulation. Charge them up till they explode under the asses of white folks, subvert their crooked miserable lives."[20] And they are anguished dreams, ending in a vision of his violent death, a symbol of his impotence in the face of white power.

The African Image can be described as Mphahlele's emotional autobiography. It tells of his mental growth. He tells us how his writing developed, the difficulties with which he had to contend. He states his credo as a black artist. "The artist must keep searching for his African personality. He can't help doing so because after all it is really a search for his own personality, for the truth about himself."[21] In the new version he makes it quite clear that he does not consider it the function of creative writers to foist their ideas on society. "They are but mere craftsmen, mere recorders, mere observers, who must take the cue from what the mass of society do, think, say and hear and dream."[22]

A large section of both versions is devoted to literary ideas and critical commentary. Both the old and the new version are divided

into two sections headed "Political Images" and "Literary Images."
Since ideas like negritude are of close concern to creative writing,
the sections are not strictly kept apart.

The literary section is an examination of the black man in
literature, and of how white and black see each other and the blacks
see themselves, through their writing. After an introductory chapter,
the nonwhite characters, as seen by white writers, are divided into
groups of images and considered under headings like "Savages,
Brutal and Noble," "The Degenerates," "Children of the
Wasteland," "The Migrant," "Man with a Halo," "The Menacing
Servants," "The Rebel," etc.

There is a danger, however, in examining literature according to a
preconceived plan, and Mphahlele falls into the trap. He reads
emotionally rather than critically, and looks at only one angle where
a particular writer or his work is concerned. As a result, his view of
literature here is out of focus. He speaks in one breath about well-
known and unknown writers. Joyce Cary's Mister Johnson and
Sylvester Stein's Staffnurse are given indiscriminately as samples of
"a crossbreed between a servant and a rebel."[23] Doris Lessing and
Nadine Gordimer are compared only in their treatment of the black
servant in their novels. Some of the writers hold little literary interest
for Mphahlele and are used merely to show an attitude of which they
are representative. Only in the first chapter does he express admiration for some writers, for the skill and greatness they show portraying
characters belonging to a cultural group outside of their own, and
not only because they have the right attitudes. He admires, as we
have seen, Conrad's ability to create characters superseding racial
and political boundaries. His creations, and those of E. M. Forster
and William Faulkner, are greater than those in African fiction, he
feels, "because they have much greater freedom of movement than
their African counterparts. They are not tethered to any sort of
didactic standard. They are not there to justify themselves, to vindicate themselves and their race." As a result, Mphahlele realizes,
"they can be carried through several emotional states and react to
different situations in various ways that indicate a development."[24]

Mphahlele has also often shown in his own creative writing that he
is not ignorant of what constitutes successful characterization, but he
seems to forget it in this commentary. His survey thus tends to
become superficial. He ignores the background to European
thought, for instance when speaking of the black man as portrayed
in early South African literature. He fails to explain the reason for

the romantic image of the black man in the writings of Thomas Pringle and Rider Haggard, except for a fleeting reference to the noble savage. He admits that he is unduly hard on Sarah Gertrude Millin, who is unpopular among black critics because of her emphasis on the evils of mixed blood leading to a degenerate people pursued by fate. He concedes that a critic who identified himself with the underdog characters of his color, as he is compelled to do, is apt to "be angry and impatient in a setup like this," a setup in which the writer or critic must "come to terms with himself in relation to his position as either one of an underdog majority or as one of a privileged minority."[25]

Thus, while it is legitimate to study the black man in fiction, it is inevitably disastrous to consider fiction solely through one aspect of this kind. The critic is bound to lose sight of literary values. There is insufficient assessment, no thesis argued and brought to a conclusion, few ideas and insights to interest the reader. Mphahlele answers the critics of his "unorthodox literary criticism"[26] in the preface to the second edition. He sees his method only as a matter of emphasis on one aspect. In a search for images via character and setting," he continues, "how could one avoid talking about other aspects of fiction where they are important?" Yet avoid it, for the most part, he does. He aimed, he says, at probing the writer's "index of value" in the context of his social milieu. Where he fails in his aim is in describing and categorizing, instead of interpreting and probing. He does not achieve his professed aim of bringing the reader closer to the intention of the novelists. His comments may not be faulty, but they are too shallow to carry the reader along.

The absence of interpretation is not quite so evident when Mphahlele turns to black writers. Here he is more at ease. He can read a novel by Alex La Guma without the barrier of irritation and suspicion, and thus find that "from all the chaos of District Six ghetto life, La Guma has hammered out a work of art that formulates a short, sharp and beautiful and effective definition of that chaos: a life of dissipation and unarticulated but dead end aspirations."[27] But then again he speaks of Richard Rive's novel *Emergency* as though it were of equal value. Both La Guma and Rive are treated in a historical survey of black South African literature under the general theme of a black urban idiom in writing. There are no guidelines for the novice reader, no indication of the critic's preference for the initiated, with which to compare his or her own. The fact that Mphahlele is looking for the black image in the name of greater racial understanding is no excuse. An image is important only for the effect it has, and surely good fiction makes more impact than bad.

Mphahlele's research into the earlier history of black South African writing, forming the basis of his academic thesis, is thorough and original. He introduces black South African literature as a "most frightening image" of "a country run on utterly false standards in every walk of life."[28] At first, he says, when black Africans began to write, they mourned the loss of idyllic tribal life, but gradually they developed an urban idiom of their own. He traces black South African literature from early religious writing, published by the mission presses, to the present day. He discusses most of the leading works, often skillfully distilling the essence of their meaning. Mhudi, main character in a novel of that name (by Sol Plaatje), for example, comes alive for him, in spite of the author's historic detachment and use of stilted dialogue, because "his love for human beings is profound."[29] He realizes that the kind of protest Peter Abrahams expresses in the novel *Path of Thunder,* where the black hero turns his wrath on a society that forbids his marriage with a white girl, limits the emotional and intellectual range of characterization.

Although Mphahlele was closely involved with other writers of the 1950's who were his colleagues on *Drum* magazine, their writing often did not appeal to him. Can Themba, the most talented of the *Drum* story contributors, he felt, cynically turned his back on life. Todd Matshikiza, sending up, as we would say today, American fiction with impish humor, he finds slickly American. Dugmore Boetie, the first black South African nonhero, he takes almost seriously. He seems to miss the irony in their fiction, by concentrating on the unlikely plots. In the new version he adds an appreciation of Themba, but it is an appreciation of the man rather than of his writing.

Summing up the state of black South African fiction at the time of writing *The African Image,* Mphahlele agrees with his compatriot Lewis Nkosi that the gargantuan reality that is South Africa makes it unexploitable as literary material. He wonders, however, whether the reality is equally inaccessible through the imagination of the poet. Poetry, after all, he says, "rushes soonest into situations that call for urgent self-expression and interpretation."[30] When considering the individual poets at the time of writing, he finds Oswald Mtshali possibly "too young to want to take a cold look at power and evaluate the pain."[31] He concedes that Mtshali is trying to understand life in his own ghetto in the conflict of social chaos, but finds his poetry too full of rhetoric and "custom-made images."[32] He finds

that Mtshali "sneaks in" his good and telling lines, and fails to see
him as a real poet whose images have impact and whose simplicity
deceptively sneaks in deep contemplation. At the time of writing,
Mtshali's *Sounds of a Cowhide Drum* had just been published in
South Africa. Since then there has been an American and a British
edition. Mphahlele finds himself more in sympathy with the poets in
exile such as Arthur Nortje, who described the isolation of exile as a
"gutted warehouse at the back of pleasure streets,"[33] and Dennis
Brutus, who feels he is driftwood, belonging nowhere but in South
Africa.

The second and third part of the section "Black on Black" deals
with black writers north of the Zambesi. Here Mphahlele is more
objective in his interpretations. "We must keep looking at it [the im-
age] in the context of the novel, in relation to the writer's intention,
tone, setting, social milieu," he says.[34] Characters in novels must
now reveal what they are like as individuals among people. The new
version differs considerably from the old, where he only mentions
these writers briefly. There is no attempt in these sections to interpret the writing in terms of "image," except for a general category
expressed in such chapter headings as "Man in Revolt," and
"Despair Disillusion Prophecy." The theme rather is the black man's
burden of responsibility to portray and interpret this.

Mphahlele feels that it is the creative writer's duty to involve
himself in the black man's present and future. His aim in *The
African Image* is to show ways toward a better understanding of the
black man. The white man must understand the black man and the
black man must understand himself. Consequently, it is necessary
for the leading black writers to become better known, especially
among black readers. Mphahlele was one of the first to work toward
the acceptance of black writers in university and school syllabuses in
black countries. He also advocates conferences and workshops. His
writing and other activities thus all point in the same direction, and
The African Image is an avowal of his life's aims. It would have been
more effective and more consistently instead of spasmodically read-
able if there had been greater discipline in organizing the contents.

II Voices in the Whirlwind and Other Essays

This volume derives its title from a poem by Gwendolyn Brooks,
who, Mphahlele feels, has a lot to teach the black man. The
whirlwind, Brooks says, "is our commonwealth," and Mphahlele explains that strife is there and must be acknowledged. Nevertheless,

he explains, "people must live," and thus, as Brooks says, "Live and go out/Define and/medicate the whirlwind," and "conduct your blooming in the noise and whip of the whirlwind."[35]

"Voices in the Whirlwind" is the title of the first essay in this collection and was specially written for the collection. All but one of the other essays were previously published in periodicals, and they continue the themes raised in *African Image*. In the first essay Mphahlele explains his concept of poetry as a balance of personal experience and a communal voice, and at the same time an ironic tension between what a poem has to express and the urge to communicate.

In the second essay he asks specifically (in the title) "African Literature: What Tradition?" and proceeds to answer the question. The third essay examines African culture in more detail, while the fourth looks at Pan-Africanism from the viewpoint of color rather than culture. The fifth essay turns to protest writing, examining the writer and his commitment, and the last one stands somewhat outside the general theme in that it deals with censorship in South Africa.

Mphahlele shows increased confidence in the treatment of his subject matter. The contents hold together more coherently, though still presented with deliberate subjectivity, and he develops his themes methodically and brings them to logical conclusions. His arguments are often crystallized into images and metaphors. In "The Fabric of African Cultures," for instance, the image of the African aesthete devoid of a synthesis of Europe and Africa, glorifying only his ancestors and celebrating African purity and innocence, is one of a continent lying in state. The difference between a writer of the negritude school — in this case Senghor — and a South African writer, he symbolizes in "African Literature: What Tradition" by their different attitude toward night. Senghor's "night of Africa" is a night teaming with suns and rainbows — "yes, there are poets who are in love with night," says Mphahlele — whereas for him night spells violence, police raids, screams. "The South African writer is always searching for daytime."[36]

Mphahlele's increased knowledge of world literature and of the theories and principles of literary criticism becomes more obvious in this work than in the second edition of *The African Image*, since it does not suffer the handicap of being a revised earlier work. His love for literature as a motivating force in his critical writing comes through more clearly. Tradition in Africa, for instance, is not an academic subject for him, but a living theme in literature. His lengthy quotations often seem selected not just to prove a point, but also to share with the reader a piece of writing worthy of being chosen. With an economy of words he succeeds in presenting the core of a literary work (for instance, the poems of Gwendolyn Brooks) and at the same time expresses the deep effect they had on him.

His writing is still often in the form of musings, but less artificially introduced than in *The African Image*. His themes and arguments are all personally felt. He gives the impression not of trying to put an argument across to convince the reader, but of examining matters that are close to his heart. "I am looking for a meaning of poetry. . . . I take up book after book that purports to show the power and use of poetry . . . I ponder the various theories about literature. . . ."[37]

When Mphahlele writes on a literary theme, he produces not so much a literary essay as a commentary on writers with whom he is closely involved intellectually. This is evident even when he discusses a writer's style. "Sometimes the words seem to come tumbling down a hill, giving you one jolt after another," he says of the black American poet, Larry Neal.[38]

The first essay, "Voices in the Whirlwind," is subtitled "Poetry and Conflict in the Black World." Mphahlele begins by analyzing what poetry means to him and how, as a teacher, he introduced methods that would enable the student to draw the same amount of pleasure from it as he did, though independently. Poetry, he says, is a heightened and condensed form of expression, available to all, since "every human being of average intelligence has poetic states of mind at different times; i.e., every person, literate or illiterate, at one time or another perceives things and events poetically. He sees something behind the initial stimulus, or meanings radiate or vibrate from the thing perceived; that what we *read* as poetry is merely the work of the literate, a sophisticated activity."

From there he leads the student to the idea of poetry as a "state of mind first." He found a novel way of demonstrating this to an adult class in Nigeria. He asked them to write down as many metaphors and proverbs as they could think up, each in the original language. Then they had to give a literal translation. "It became clear to the class," Mphahlele says, "that each time a person uttered such a speech in everyday life, it was either in circumstances of ritual or it was a way of lending gravity or importance to what was being said, even in humorous circumstances. The speaker would be wanting to

strike at more meanings than one at any time. There was a conscious
or unconscious attempt to synthesize, to see things as a whole, made
up of interconnected elements."[39]

Since poetry is a state of mind, Mphahlele tells us, it "tends to be a
ready tool for the expression or dramatization of protest and indignation and exhortation for many who regard themselves as poets."[40]
He explores African and Afro-American poetry against a background
of modern European thought, as represented mainly by the critical
writings of Christopher Caudwell,[41] I. A. Richards,[42] and Laurence
Lerner.[43] A work of art, Mphahlele insists, must both express the artist's personal emotions and communicate these to the reader. At the
same time it must integrate and unify this personal experience and
the sum of experience of his fellowmen. "Great art," he continues,
"thus endures because it integrates private instincts with those common to man in general within a cultural context."[44] If both these
aspects are not accepted, the immediate and the universal — what
Gwendolyn Brooks calls the "two-headed responsibility" — there
can be no real art, he concludes.

Mphahlele finds that his ideas are still irreconcilable with
negritude as a modern cultural force. He feels that there is no need
for conflict in the critic's mind whether to adhere to Western values
or to reject or suspend them. The standard that he uses in reviewing
black poetry is an aesthetic he considers basic to poetry, and should
thus be acceptable to all. This aesthetic provides poetry that com-
municates a communal voice through an individual experience or a
unique private emotion. This implies balance. He criticizes Claude
McKay, the black American poet, for instance, for his apparent
overemphasis on the universal aspect in some of his poetry, thus
diminishing his immediate appeal to his black audience. He con-
trasts this with the poems of Gwendolyn Brooks, who builds up a picture of conflict by capturing the various facets of an experience.

Although Mphahlele, as a South African black man, born and bred
in the white man's *apartheid* world, finds it difficult to accept a
separate black aesthetic, he feels he must at least show tolerance
toward these new ideas. He explains them as a withdrawing of a
black minority from white standards, just as in South Africa the
black man was driven to create his own cultural innovations in the
ghettos. But he remains sceptical about the rejection of the Western
system of aesthetics. Just what is it that is to be rejected, he wants to
know. Is emotion culturally based, he asks, and answers: "Perhaps in
the acting it out, yes."[45] If an ethnic aesthetic is to evolve, it will, he

feels, be through the theater, an aesthetic such as we find in blues, jazz, soul, music, the rhythm of dance, and independent Negro religious worship.

And what is it that makes up Western culture, he enquires, what are its components, and is it really exclusively Western? It is, after all, itself fragmented and has been challenged throughout its existence. Mphahlele warns against the danger of dismissing the Western aesthetic "Out of sheer crusading zeal,"[46] thus dismissing elements which are "built into our new modes of expression."[47] Nothing, he feels, has really so far emerged from the black world other than a black point of view.

Having examined American Negro poetry in the context of commitment in conflict, Mphahlele studies, for the purpose of comparison, African poets in three areas: French-speaking Africa, South Africa, and the independent English-speaking states. For him the important black South African poets in 1972 are still those living abroad, men like Dennis Brutus, who actively as well as in their poetry oppose the South African government.

As an exile himself, Mphahlele was unable to foresee or to appreciate the importance of poets living in South Africa, such as Oswald Mtshali and Wally Serote, who represent the new voice — a strong and independent voice — of the black man in oppression. According to Mtshali, who consciously follows the tradition of the Zulu, labels like "protest poetry" are imposed by the whites and are meaningless to him as a poet. He himself must write from his own experience. "We have lost the heritage of our Bantu poetry which spoke a metaphor and allegory that were native to us," says Mphahlele.[48] Mtshali, author of *Cowhide Drum*, declared to a white audience that he would henceforth write in Zulu, since his people did not attend academic poetry readings, but listened to Radio Bantu.

Mphahlele predicts that South African poetry will follow Afro-American protest writing more and more, and quotes Keorapetse Kgositsile, a South African living in the United States, as an example. He senses, however, that the successful South African poets are writing with a sense of faith in the future, a confidence in the eventual outcome of the conflict in a country where the blacks have an overwhelming majority. Thus, in the writing of Dennis Brutus, he sees the images of oppression grind and flash and sparkle, but knows that the ordinary human tenderness survives.

Mphahlele makes little comment on conflict in French African poetry, where he chooses David Diop as its representative. He finds the independent English-speaking states of Africa a more difficult area than South Africa, when examining poetry in relation to conflict. Soyinka, in his revolt against the sanctification of authority, seems the most successful exponent of a synthesis of the personal and the communal.

Mphahlele comes to no cut-and-dried conclusion in this essay. He feels he dare not answer categorically the question as to whether there is a black aesthetic in poetry. Such an aesthetic, he says, fails to account for everyone's ability to respond positively to heightened emotion or suggested meaning in art, a response that cannot possibly be dependent on one's racial group, unless one raises the barrier oneself.

In the second essay, "African Literature: What Tradition?" originally published in the *Denver Quarterly*,[49] Mphahlele studies the type of art practiced in Africa before the coming of the white man. The purpose, or impetus of such art, he emphasizes, was always a spiritual one. Such art, he says, is comprehensible only to those who appreciate and understand the impulses that operate within a particular cult. This does not apply to the African today, and thus the preservation of African culture becomes artificial. Any attempt to push the African into a separate niche is achieved either by the white man for his own political ends, as in South Africa, or by the black man himself as a negative reaction, a revulsion against Europe, as in French-speaking Africa, or against the white man in the United States. If, however, the black artist is left to himself, the results could be astounding. Who knows, Mphahlele says, "we may yet see tradition accounted for, not necessarily directly through the art that stands at some remove in the past. It may sneak in from the area of verbal arts and craftwork."[50]

Mphahlele is no longer so sure that the choice of a European language is a wise one. By using the language of the colonizer, the writer is abandoning the route leading from tradition because his idiom is no longer that of the people he is writing about. His writing often becomes an intellectual projection, deliberately directed toward a white audience.

Mphahlele answers the question he asks in the essay title: "Tradition in Africa is not, as in the Western world, made up of centuries or eras telescoping into one another. Rather, it consists of various patches of landscape with several common features."[51] What these are he explains in the third essay, "Fabric of African Cultures," previously published in *Foreign Affairs* (July, 1964.) He lists the broad elements of African culture common to most of the societies on the continent: the place of the extended family in the social structure, the sense of communal responsibility, the tendency to gravitate toward other people rather than toward things and places, reverence for ancestral spirits, and audience participation in entertainment activities. These, he says, make up the African personality. He no longer sees tradition as lost, but finds evidence of a line of continuity in the culture of the South African black townships, virile because of a happy superimposition of Western culture on African tradition.

He begins the essay by quoting the type of lyric sung by dancers before a township wedding. It is a sad song, in which a boy tries to entice a girl to lose herself in shanty town, "tin-and-sack-town." The slums have given birth to the song, but the music and the wedding itself are based on tradition. At the end of the essay Mphahlele reaffirms that, whatever the conditioning factors in African cultural development, the African wants to "determine his cultural organization himself."[52]

Having studied the African from the cultural point of view, Mphahlele now turns to an examination of color as a unifying force. In "Implications of Color Identity in Pan-Africa," he traces the history of Pan-Africanism and wonders just what part color plays in the African's self-identification. He comes to no conclusion, feeling that the emphasis on color as such is a pose. In this essay he sees the African personality as based on something more abstract than the codes of tradition listed in the previous essay. The African way of life, he says, is centered on the urge to be, a love of life as an end itself.

Once again he explains his rejection of negritude. In case anyone should think that his support of Western culture as a beneficial influence is synonymous with support of white colonialism, he explains that without contact with colonialism, the changes brought about by Western civilization and culture would still have taken place, but might have been directed and controlled by the Africans themselves.

"African Writers and Commitment" originally appeared as "Writers and Commitment" in *Black Orpheus*. In this essay Mphahlele tells us that every writer "is committed to something beyond his art" to a statement of value not purely aesthetic, to a "criticism of life."[53] He examines Jean-Paul Sartre's contention that literature must be made to serve a political purpose, concluding that this insistence on social and political programs appears altogether too rigid. "Can Sartre's kind of discipline and aims for literature become inviolable rules for a craft that is always breaking rules, breaking down myths?" he asks.[54] Especially where African literature is concerned, Mphahlele finds this functional meaning a dangerous tendency since it can limit the author's vision.

Mphahlele then demonstrates various forms of commitment in African literature, without, as he says, attempting "to be categorical about whether propaganda should or should not enter a work of art."[55] He does not feel that this is important; "rather it is the manner in which the writer uses propaganda that decides the literary worth of a work."[56] He quotes Tolstoi's remarks in *Literature and Revolution* about the necessity of the Russian proletariat to express in art the new spiritual point of view, then says he would like to think that African negritude propaganda has prompted, similarly, the need to search for a new spiritual point of view; not a black pride that drugs the black man into a condition of stupor or inertia, but one which continues to see the African hero in an integrated communal world, as opposed to the Western literary hero of a Kafka or a Camus, stricken with *angst* and dashing about like a trapped fly.

The last essay, "Censorship in South Africa," was published in the first anniversary issue of *Censorship Today: A Review of the Continuing Fight for Free Speech*. It is a factual, if bitter, account of censorship in South Africa, a system that curtails intellectual freedom. He explains the workings and effects of two laws, the Publications and Entertainment Act and the Amendment to the Suppression of Communism Act, under which the Government controls and directs political thinking. He also explains how the Bantu Education Act serves as a form of censorship, since no black teacher, even in his private capacity, may write or utter any kind of criticism of any public servant. It was for campaigning against this act that Mphahlele was dismissed from teaching by the South African Government.

II Other Essays *and Critical Writing*

In Mphahlele's uncollected essays and in his lectures the same themes are raised as in the collections. Many of the important journals of three continents have asked him to contribute, and his presence as a speaker at conferences and as a visiting lecturer at universities is much sought after.

Often, again, we find Mphahlele discussing the conflict between the universal in literature and a specifically black aesthetic. In "Why

I Teach my Discipline" he explains why his viewpoint, from the literary aspect, differs from that of Afro-Americans: "Since coming to the United States I have discovered how passionately students discuss ideas and the social milieu of a writer even before they have exposed themselves fully to the language in the text. In Africa, the teacher tends more often to rely on the language and on correspondences between, say, an English situation and an African one — or lack of correspondence."[57] When studying Wordsworth's "I Wandered Lonely as a Cloud," for instance, the important thing was not that an African did not know a daffodil, but what the daffodils did to Wordsworth in vacant or in pensive mood. Mphahlele continues:

What will be the all-important thing is the fact that an African would never contemplate nature the way Wordsworth did. In rural life we are surrounded so much by nature that it ceases to be something outside ourselves. We are part of its rhythm. Its birth is our birth, its death ours, its stagnation or suspension ours. In the city we are too happy to have escaped the bleakness of the rural landscape, the cruelties of external nature, its rules of survival, to feel nostalgic about it.[58]

This comparison arises out of the text of Wordsworth's poem. In America, Mphahlele says, all students want to do is to discuss ideas. "They don't really care how these ideas are expressed in the text. They refuse to read a poem aloud, so that they hear the ring of words. They skim through a novel and rush to read what the critics say about it."[59] This "continuous process of plundering literary works for ideas about society they may yield, until the creative text becomes unimportant"[60] appalls him.

The reason for his different approach he attributes to the different background from which he came to English literature, one in which he had to find meaning in the writing for himself, where his early love was not due to the encouragement or help he received from teachers but "*had* to be self-generated."[61] He had to find answers to his own questions, and this produced in him "an ingrained habit of mind, which is to read a text closely even before one contemplates the ideas that inform the literature."[62]

He explains what he means by place, an expression he often uses in the context of commitment. One cannot, he says, glean ideas from a superficial reading of literature and use them to promote action in a different place. African literature, he implies — to put it plainly — cannot be used to promote Third World power in America.

130 EZEKIEL MPHAHLELE

With the greater discipline required by an isolated essay, Mphahlele often sees his themes more clearly and expresses them more succinctly than in his other works. He explains why he teaches his discipline, English literature and especially African literature in English, in the essay of that title, as follows:

A literature is growing in Africa produced in English. At this level I teach for the following reasons: to promote a vehicle of communication among ourselves across diverse cultural and ethnic boundaries; to discover ourselves through a medium that combines an African sensibility with an English mode of expression; to discover ourselves through an understanding of the meeting point between imitation and innovation; the meeting point between two cultures, one of which stimulates and releases the creative energies of the other. I have been in the center of these processes. Studying and teaching literature has been part of that process of expansion from the mastery of reading and writing skills to higher levels of consciousness.[63]

Always he uses concrete examples from literature rather than theories. When taking American students to task for indulging in "talk, talk, talk" about a literary work instead of going to the text, he says:

Try asking Huckleberry Finn what he thinks of the frontier mentality of America; ask him if he thinks dedicating himself to helping a runaway slave is an escape from civilization, back to one's beginnings. Questions like these some people worry about. Huck is likely to make a bolt for it, back into the novel, for protection. Back into the novel which is the house Mark Twain built for him. . . . Herein lies the beauty of a work of art: every time you try to dissect it, the spirit of the whole keeps reclaiming the parts and the thing is together again, even though the whole tempts one to dissect it.[64]

Mphahlele's comments are always distinguished by their honesty and integrity. For him the greatest crime a writer can commit is false posturing, striking a pose, peddling in dogma, sloganizing, and indulging in intellectual snobbery, while his highest praise is for a writer who maintains a balance between artistic integrity and commitment. Except for the work based on his student thesis, he refuses to base his discussions on any subject on a preconceived notion, and he is not interested in discussing any theme unless he is deeply involved in it.

Mphahlele does not write about literature as a professional critic. When he chooses to discuss Langston Hughes, for instance, he does so because he loves his poetry. In his essay "Langston Hughes"[65] he allows Hughes to speak for himself a great deal. Hughes appeals to him because he does not take himself too seriously, and because of his boundless zest for life. He appreciates Hughes' refusal to write of primitive African things under the sponsorship of a wealthy white woman and his rejection of African rhythms used as a purely theoretical and romantic measure. Hughes, according to Mphahlele, has found his "place." He was not of Africa, but of Chicago and Kansas City and Broadway and Harlem.

Mphahlele's aim as a critic is always to bring us closer to the writer's intentions. Throughout, however, runs his search for literature that fulfills what he considers its highest aim, the search for "truth that lives in an historical context," that seeks "beauty in man, that thing in man which has permanence and stands the test of political change."[66]

His love for literature and joy in teaching it comes through again and again. In an essay entitled "Black Literature at the University of Denver" he tells us how, in a course in African literature, he changed the prescribed works from time to time "for one's own edification and interest as a lecturer."[67] "Teaching is my vocation," he declares in "Why I Teach my Discipline." "On my own terms I do nothing else as successfully."[68] Even in his novel *The Wanderers* his counterpart enjoys teaching and is always innovating, exploring, finding reasons for poor performance. It was mainly Timi/Mphahlele's frustration as a teacher that drove him out of Iboyoru/Nigeria. He had suggestions for improvement in adult education, but could not get his superiors to discuss them.

And yet, sometimes even in Nigeria, he yearned for the response, the lack of complacency, of his South African students:

In the south the boys and I were caught up in a violent situation. We both carried a pass and we could be stopped and searched or arrested the moment we stepped out of the school grounds. We were both hungering for many things and getting little, which in turn sharpened the edge of our longings. I responded to every throb of pain and restlessness in them, and I think they responded to my yearnings.[69]

He told Dennis Duerden, in an interview at a conference on African Literature in University Curricula at Fourah Bay College, Freetown, that teaching as a whole is appallingly out of touch with reality and that, while literature can be a discipline, it must never be out of touch with life. At this conference he emphasized once again that, while teaching of African literature must increase at African univer-

sities, students must also be exposed to the various good and
meaningful literatures of the world. He warned against building a
ghetto around literature, a literary Bantustan.

The scope of Mphahlele's critical writing and his public lectures
appears limited. He speaks of his love for European English
literature, yet he rarely writes or speaks about the actual writing.
The fault is probably not his. As an authority on African English
literature this is the subject he is asked to write and lecture about. In
his own classes he doubtless becomes deeply involved with other
literary subjects.

In his most recent essays Mphahlele seems defensive about his
principles; sometimes it is almost as though he has been driven
against a wall and has to defend himself against the onslaught of
those among whom he is exiled. We feel that he is confused by the
new political developments in independent Africa and by the
strivings of Black Power in America, with which he would like to
identify, yet finds it impossible to do so. A note of uncertainty has
crept into his style, and as a result there is the acknowledged loss of
place, perhaps even loss of foothold, in his critical writing as well as
in his most recent fiction. It lacks his previous vitality.

Although Mphahlele is still recognized as an authority on African
writing everywhere, lately there have been dissident voices. He was
attacked for his point of view as early as 1962, after the publication
of *The African Image*. In the *West African Review* I. Tagbo Nwogu
accused him of compromising and of lacking profundity in analysis.
While he respected Mphahlele's criticism, he called him unrepresen-
tative of independent Africa. A year later Mphahlele complained at a
conference of African Literature in French and the Universities, held
at the University of Dakar in March, 1963, that his body itched from
the number of labels that had been stuck on him. He felt he was being misunderstood, that his black critics felt he was spurning African
tradition. Yet it was he, in 1960, who replied to Dan Jacobson, when
the white South African writer living in London said that African
history began with the invasion of the white man, and what civilization there might have been had lapsed out of the consciousness of
the race. Replying[70] to Jacobson's essay "Out of Africa,"[71]
Mphahlele points out that there is in the oral literature of African
nations a considerable body of history which indicates very clearly
the moral and social codes that governed the lives of people a very
long time ago. He declares that he is deeply conscious of where he
falls in this long line of continuity among the Bantu-speaking

peoples of Africa. He is keenly aware of what is valuable in African traditional culture. What he emphasizes, though, is that the African should be allowed to choose what he wishes to retain of the Western culture he has adopted. In a more humorous vein, he told a television interviewer that he himself has no sleepless nights wondering if he will eat or dress African the next day. His African values continue to remain a solid thing inside him: the African humanism and the sense of wanting to be one with a community. His individualism, he feels, is the European part of him.

In 1963 he was engaged in a controversy over the use of English as a creative vehicle for Africans in the readers' pages of *Transition*. He did not always find it a pleasurable experience, he remarked, to be in the position of a fullback in literary arguments. In the 1970's he is in the defense line once again. The field this time is the United States and the goal of the opposing side is a black art where the criterion for a melody, a play, or a poem is not how beautiful it is but how much more beautiful it makes the life of the black man.

Reviewing *Voices in the Whirlwind* in *Blackworld*, Addison Gayle, Jr., strongly takes issue with Mphahlele for paying tribute to the West for bringing civilization to Africa. Gayle questions the value of Western civilization by claiming that history disproves its humanistic basis. Although he finds *Voices* a "moving critical document," he finds Mphahlele under a delusion in seeing Western civilization as "both bitch goddess and desirable maiden."[72] Mphahlele, replying in the January, 1974, issue of the same journal, finds Gayle's review "the most damaging indictment I have ever been put through." He feels that Gayle has constructed an image of him as "a kind of Afro-Saxon or Euro-African who can't be trusted to speak for Africa."[73] He finds Gayle's attitude toward Africa utopian and unrealistic. Mphahlele, always tolerant and polite, obviously does not want to be too explicit in pointing out the absurdity of the accusation that he, of Africa by birth, language, custom, and parentage, must prove himself an African. Sadly, he wonders whether communication has broken down.

III   *Anthologies*

In view of Mphahlele's keen interest in promoting African writing, it is natural that sooner or later he would want to collect some of this writing to share with others. He has thus produced one anthology of his own and co-edited another. As a teacher, lecturer, and one-time fiction editor of *Drum*, the selection of works he considered worth reading was, of course, nothing new for him. Like his commentaries, his collections emphasize, as he tells us in the introduction to *African Writing Today*, the major universal concerns in literature, interpreted in African terms. The introduction to the other anthology, *Modern African Stories*, which he co-edited with Ellis Ayitey Komey, is not signed, but Mphahlele's voice is clear in it. What is it, the editors ask, that is responsible for the spurt of literary activity in Western Africa as opposed to South Africa, Rhodesia, and Kenya? The answer, they say, lies in the impact of Western education and institutions which were "just powerful enough to make them look back, soberly and no longer ashamed as a group, into their past and the societies they come from."[74] This distinguishes it from French-speaking West Africa, which "speaks the language of an *élite* and is preoccupied only with its sense of loss and other concerns which are not felt by the majority of Africans."[75] It is the theme of synthesis which Mphahlele reiterates, but here demonstrates by publishing stories by West Africans full of local color and themes, some expressing "the strange twists of irony we experience in the fatalism of Africa,"[76] many others dealing with the conflict between old and new.

The South African stories, on the other hand, illustrate mainly protest writing, which, the editors tell us, is produced by the challenge of socio-political life. The writing of black South Africans, the editors say, is "full of sensuous imagery, impressionism, anger, impatience, because they are always groping for a medium whereby they and their own immediate audience . . . can come to terms with a world of physical and mental violence, of dispossession, and with a world in which they are called upon to assert their human dignity."[77] In this collection the editors have no axe to grind. Mphahlele and Komey make no claim for "*un style negro-africain*." There is no attempt to press a point.

We do not know whether the authors worked independently, each making his own choice, but it is likely that Mphahlele chose the South African stories. The publishers insisted that the editors include their own stories, and Mphahlele chose one of his best, "Greig on a Stolen Piano." Most of the leading South African fiction writers are represented: Alex La Guma ("Coffee for the Road"), James Matthews ("The Second Coming"), Richard Rive ("Rain"), and Can Themba ("The Dube Train"). Although the title indicates that *Modern African Stories* is a collection of stories, an extract from Alfred Hutchinson's *Road to Ghana*, under the title "Machado," and a sketch from Casey Motsisi's *Drum* series "On the Beat" are included. Items from other areas also include extracts, such as "Death of a Boy," which is taken from Chinua Achebe's novel *Things Fall Apart*, and extracts from Amos Tutuola's *Feather Woman of the Jungle*.

The whole gamut of African themes and problems is represented in this collection. The boy in James Ngugi's story "A Meeting in the Dark" is caught helplessly between the Christian fanaticism of his father, who expects him to take up a scholarship, and custom, which expects him to marry the circumcised girl he has made pregnant. The boy kills the girl and thus destroys himself for both worlds. "The Blood in the Washbasin" by William Conton proves that the African in the black man needs no constant affirmation, since it will affirm itself. Kelfah, in this story, tries to deny it, when, as the first black master of a mailship, he laughs politely with the Europeans, who tell about a sailor who playfully fired harpoons at an African's canoe. Kelfah knows that the African in the story was his own grandfather and that he later died of gangrene caused by the harpoon wound. When about to land, something explodes within Kelfah, and he directs the ship full speed ahead into the dock.

Apartheid and its various problems is obviously the main theme of the South African contributions. They are a good cross section of the dramatic, as in James Matthews' story "The Second Coming," about a shepherd who thought he had been chosen to lead oppressed black farm workers to freedom; the satiric, in Casey Motsisi's sketches about South African politics and social life ; the stark realism of the South African scene in the stories by Alex La Guma, Alfred Hutchinson, and Richard Rive about clashes between black and white; and the cynicism of Can Themba, which usually does not appeal to Mphahlele but which he realizes he must include to make the collection completely representative of South African writing in that section.

The other anthology, *African Writing Today*,[78] again has no professed theme other than to reflect Africa's awareness of itself. It is meant as a survey, a "map of themes and styles." Mphahlele includes as many important writers as possible, explaining omissions, which he lists, as economy. In his introduction he also explains that, rather than include works easily available elsewhere, he has chosen several new authors and less well-known works of established writers. He divides the work into areas. There is more emphasis in this work on the authors themselves. At the end are biographical

notes on the writers, giving their careers, publications, and present
places of residence.

Once again the African themes are well illustrated. An extract
from Achebe's *Arrow of God* shows the conflict between old and new
in Nigeria. Abioseh Nicol's "Life is Sweet at Kumasenu" is on the
surface a ghost story, but it is also a dramatization of the idea of continuity of life, with emphasis on the positive aspect of life itself, we
are told in the introduction to this story.

The contents are varied and include some of Africa's finest
writing. There are poems, short stories, extracts from plays and from
novels. The extracts have been carefully selected to stand on their
own. That from Wole Soyinka's "The Swamp Dwellers," for instance, is an exciting scene from a powerful play. There is an ade-
quate introduction to each extract, but unless necessary to the understanding, there is no summary of the whole work. Mphahlele, the
teacher, thus makes sure that the reader goes to the original work
and does not use the anthology as a meaningless academic aid!

Another satisfying extract is that from Amos Tutuola's *My Life in
the Bush of Ghosts.* Less well known than *The Palm Wine Drinkard,*
it has the same fascination. This extract, against a background of
folklore, tells the exciting story of a man married to a ghost and how
he eventually returns to his people. Mphahlele, in the introduction,
points to the deeper meaning of this journey, leading from innocence to knowledge.

An extract from Camara Laye's *The Radiance of the King* is introduced by explaining the symbolic meaning of the novel, and then
an incident, interesting in itself, is given to illustrate this. Here
Mphahlele does recount the plot briefly. Nearly all the well-known
poets are represented, including some in translation, such as
Tchikaya U'Tam'si, David Diop, Senghor, and Lenrie Peters. There
are stories by writers from the Portuguese-speaking territories, including Luis Bernardo Honwana, on of black Africa's best short story
writers, whose work was little known in English at the time.

Of his own works, Mphahlele includes two essays, one entitled
"Remarks on Negritude," which he presented as a paper at a conference on African Literature in French at the Universities, held at
the University of Dakar, March, 1963, and which voices his usual
stand on this issue; and an extract from an article published in *Encounter* entitled "An African Autobiography," about his stay in
Nigeria.

The South Africa section contains one of Alex La Guma's best stories, "Blankets," Richard Rive's story "Dagga-Smoker's Dream," and Can Themba's "The Urchin." The latter is the violent and melodramatic type of story of Themba's that Mphahlele disliked, but again felt necessary to include, especially as it had won a prize in a contest organized by the South African Centre of the International Pen Club. There are poems by Dennis Brutus and Mazisi Kunene, Lewis Nkosi's searingly satiric story, "The Prisoner," and an extract from Todd Matshikiza's *Chocolates for my Wife*. All these contributions help to fulfill the main function of an anthology: to preserve writing that is worth reading.

CHAPTER 7

The Wanderers

IN August, 1968, shortly after Mphahlele had finished writing his novel *The Wanderers* he was interviewed by Cosmo Pieterse at the Studio Transcription Centre of the British Broadcasting Corporation in London.[1] In this discussion of his writing Mphahlele described his first volume, *Man Must Live*, as a clumsy piece of writing and something he would not want to read again. His Newclare series in *Drum*, however, he told Pieterse, he would like to resuscitate. Speaking about his later stories, he described "Mrs. Plum" as a kind of finger exercise to see what he could make of the long story or novella. It gave him confidence to tackle a novel, he said. *The Wanderers* was the result.

Mphahlele felt that he was ready for book-length fiction. He must also have realized that the literary climate was right for it. When he wrote *Down Second Avenue* and the short stories, he was writing as an unknown black man for a mainly white readership in South Africa and Britain. Now his book would find a world market as the work of an important African writer. Thus, whatever he had to say would have to be said fully. His concerns would have to be the concerns of Africa on a larger canvas. Clash of color, the main subject of black writers from South Africa, which would not have sufficed him in any case, was no longer enough. He would have to stand beside other African novelists of the stature of Achebe, Laye, Ekwensi, and Okara, men who dealt with more subtle, sophisticated, and complicated problems.

Africa and its interaction with the displaced author is the theme of *The Wanderers*. Mphahlele told Cosmo Pieterse that it was the first time he had tried to give a panoramic view of Africa and the torments that Africa was going through. "If *The Wanderers* says anything at all, it should . . . be a personal record of [a] search for place,"[2] Mphahlele wrote elsewhere. "I wanted to bring out the life

of exile and put myself as the central character at different points,"
he told his interviewer at the University of Texas recently.[3] Yet he
insisted that it is more fiction than autobiography since it has an
imaginary plot and a beginning and ending.

Thus, since we are asked to regard *The Wanderers* as a novel, we
must begin by examining the story it tells. We know that the central
character, Timi Tabane, is Mphahlele, but we must remember that
The Wanderers, as the plural of the title indicates, is not just the
story of one man. It is not only Timi who has been displaced, but also
his wife and family and some of his friends, both black and white.

The story opens to the news of the death of Timi's eldest son,
Felang. He, along with twenty-six other African nationalist guerillas,
had been captured by a commando of white farmers on the borders
of Zimbabawe and thrown to the crocodiles. We gather that this
tragedy in the novel is an end as well as a beginning, not just the
physical end of one of the characters, but the conclusion of the story,
which is to be built up within its framework. It is indicated that there
has been an estrangement between Felang and his parents, and that
the relationship between Felang and his father will provide the plot.
Karabo, grieving over the loss of her son, says to her husband:

"Remember what you used to say during our trying times with Felang?"
"What in particular?"
"You said . . . , A child will wrench himself free of a parent's love and by so
doing, drive it to sleep. Then some event will rekindle it, but it may be an
event that makes the love futile, like a dead river, unnecessary; the event
may place the child out of reach."[4]

We are also introduced to Timi's white South African friend, Steven
Cartwright, who confirms the news of Felang's death after he has
reported on the event for his newspaper. We are told that Timi's and
Steven's lives twined round each other.

The narrative then switches to a much earlier period, which Timi,
as narrator, describes as the beginning, and which takes place before
the birth of Felang. The entire first of five parts is an account of
Timi's life and hardships in the township, and of his work on the
magazine *Bongo*, closely following Mphahlele's life during the
equivalent period of his career.

Timi has left teaching to join the magazine *Bongo* in the city of
Tirong. He talks about his life in the slum much as Mphahlele does
in *Down Second Avenue*, describing its "screams and sirens and
police whistles and the roar and grating of bus engines and the rattle

of electric trains and the smell of smog;"⁵ and depicting the people living there, amid the misery and violence, who try to maintain their humaneness, dignity, and sometimes humor.

Timi is as unhappy in his work for *Bongo* as Mphahlele was in his job on *Drum*. There is a nagging void within him. One day Timi is introduced to a young woman, Naledi, who believes that her husband has been shanghaied for slave labor on a farm. She asks Timi to investigate as a *Bongo* reporter. This would not be the first time that *Bongo* exposed that wicked practice, whereby, after minor offences, men and boys would be sent by the police to work on farms, usually for long periods and under incredibly bad conditions.

Timi becomes deeply involved in Naledi's problem, "much more deeply than a journalist thinks he can afford to."⁶ They journey to Goshen where the husband is rumored to have been sent. There, with false identities and the help of contacts, they settle down in a village district. Timi obtains a job with a farmer and makes enquiries about Naledi's husband, Rampa. He eventually discovers that Rampa had indeed worked there and that, as a result of a savage beating, he had been seriously injured and consequently dismissed. Later they find proof of his death.

Timi is attracted to Naledi while living with her in the village, but remains faithful to his wife, Karabo. They return, and Timi's colleagues later describe his *Bongo* story about the case as "terrific." Some prisoners are released as a result, but legal injustices continue in South Africa and Timi feels more frustrated than ever. The abduction case postpones for a while Timi's dilemma as to whether he should accept an offer to leave the country of his birth and work in Iboyoru. He knows that he will have to decide eventually "whether to stay and try to survive; or stay and pit my heroism against the machine and bear the consequences if I remained alive; or stay and shrivel up with bitterness; or face up to my cowardice, reason with it and leave."⁷ As a result of his *Bongo* story about farm slave labor, his passport application is refused.

Book Two is narrated by Steven Cartwright, white editor of *Bongo*. Steven's dilemma is that of a man with a conscience, in a country ruled by what he calls "white Thugs" and "Nazi-headed hoodlums." He, too, vacillates between responsibility and dissociation, and battles with his feelings of guilt. Steven's account of events also continues the story of Timi. We learn that Timi decided not to wait for a passport any longer, but crossed the border to the north illegally. We also get flashback glimpses of Timi during his career as a journalist, while Steven tells about his own. The rambling account is explained by the fact that Steven is ill in bed with a back complaint and his thoughts wander as he jots down notes.

Steven falls in love with Naledi, while trying to bring to an end an affair with a white novelist, Sheila Shulameth. He procures a job for Naledi as a cook in the home of friends. Although Naledi is well educated, she has no teacher's certificate and would earn less as an unqualified teacher than she would as a servant. There were no other jobs for black women in the cities at that time. Steven tells her of his love, but she has only one answer: "You are white, Mr. Cartwright."[8]

Trouble flares up in the district where Naledi's parents live when the people riot in protest against black women having to carry passes. Naledi's father is arrested. Steven reports the events for *Bongo* and Naledi, who has returned to be with her parents, stays on to help feed the victims and dress their wounds. One of the police constables calls her from her work on a pretext and takes her to a church where he attempts to seduce her by promising to set her father free. When she refuses, he tries to rape her, but she manages to escape. She lays a charge against the constable and he is found guilty, but given a suspended sentence and not dismissed from the force.

There is no narrator for the third book, which takes place two years later. We are transferred to another part of Africa where there is also trouble. The military have taken over in Iboyoru where sporadic fighting occurred. This we learn from a discussion between the famous writer, Kofi Awoonor, and Timi, who has been living in Iboyoru since he left South Africa. He had driven to the border of Botswana with a friend, crossed it on foot at a weak point, and walked to Francistown. From there an anti-South African organization had helped him to Zambia. He had applied to the Iboyoru government for a teaching post and they had flown him to the district of Sogali. Karabo had obtained an exit permit for herself and their two children and had followed six months later.

The trouble in Iboyoru brings Steven Cartwright, who has been living in England and working for a news magazine. He tells them the news that Naledi has agreed to marry him. Except for one or two casual brief scenes, it is only now — halfway through Book Three, and less than a third from the end of the novel — that we meet Felang, Mphahlele's eldest son. Timi and family move to another district, where Timi has a new teaching post and Felang is taken to boarding school. Felang proves to be a difficult child. On the way to school, Timi tries to talk to him about his education, but is met with silence or monosyllabic replies. Felang comes to hate boarding school and its discipline and refuses to apply himself to his work. Later he does no better at day school. Karabo feels that the boy needs tougher handling, but Timi hates to discipline him. They are both at a loss to understand why Felang is so difficult. "What's *eating* the boy?" Karabo asks again and again. Could it be, as the principal suggests, that he hates white people? He had witnessed one or two clashes as a boy in South Africa, and his father had taught him to spit if he saw a white policeman. Their troubles with the boy remain unsolved.

The fourth book is once more narrated by Timi. They have now moved to Lao-Kiku, as Timi was becoming restless. He was not getting the cooperation he needed in his attempts to improve education in the northern districts of Iboyoru. He could not feel sufficiently involved. "I want to work *with* people, not *for* them"[9] he writes to Steven.

Felang continues to give his parents cause for concern. Whenever he comes home from boarding school there is money missing. Timi discovers that he has stolen and sold clothes. He admits to experimenting with drugs. One morning Timi and Karabo find a note saying: "Dear Mom and Dad, I've left. I'm not going to school any more. I'll rough it alone. I won't tell you where I'm going, Felang."[10] However, he returns after a while and goes back to school. After some brief improvement, relations continue to deteriorate. Felang now mixes mainly with white and Indian boys and looks down on black Africans. Finally he leaves home again, this time for good.

Soon Timi and his family are on the move again: Timi's work permit has not been renewed. The reason given is Africanization — replacement by local teachers — but it is Timi who must go and not his white colleagues. Timi is disillusioned with Africa, having heard, for instance, that in Zambia there is an exodus of black South African teachers and nurses who are being replaced by whites. He feels he must move out of the continent and stay out until he feels he is needed, until the "waspish imperialism" — as personified for him by Miss Graves, the head of the English department where he taught, who sneered at his non-British credentials — and the "mute arrogance" of the conservative African have been replaced. Then Africa would come into its own, "a land of theatre, gaiety, of hot humid days and grey harmattans, of warm rain showers. Cities with vibrant night life."[11] Yes, he says, he might return to Iboyoru. But not now. He had expected a "roar of triumph, the triumph of black rule."[12] Instead, there had been the plaintive sound of defeat.

The book ends by recounting Felang's death and the events that led to it. He had joined the Army of Liberation in Tanzania. The Congress of Liberation had asked for Timi's approval; Timi had replied: "I don't think there's any point refusing." Felang had gone against orders that scheduled his company's entry into battle for a later date, breaking away to join a company already in action. Finally, in the Epilogue we hear that Steven Cartwright has been killed during skirmishes in the Congo, where he was reporting for an international radio network. Naledi decides to stay in London and plans to study nutrition, with her father-in-law's help.

Two things will emerge from the bare outline of the story: that it follows Mphahlele's life closely, and that the plot is a very thin thread to carry a novel of more than three hundred pages. Since it begins and ends with the death of Felang and since Mphahlele tells us the novel is concerned with a search for place, we must interpret the story of Felang as symbolic of young Africa's search for identity, and his martyrdom and death as a vindication of its aspirations. We are given a further clue about the significance of the youth theme in Timi's recurring dream of terror. In it he is pursued, but the faces of his pursuers elude him. Only toward the end of the story does he recognize them: "I did not know them individually, but I knew them to be black South Africans. Young men. They could not have been more than six or so in number. . . ."[13] Timi as a father, and Timi as narrator of events, is burdened — both as an individual and as an educated and articulate representative of his race — with an over-whelming sense of responsibility for future generations.

Within the framework of his own life story and a loosely woven and rambling account of real and imaginary characters, their wanderings, and their relations with each other, Mphahlele uses this novel as a vehicle for all the themes that have concerned him through the years of exile. He states his beliefs more clearly here than in any of his earlier works. His religious philosophy is based on traditional African humanism, a philosophy that teaches its followers to "seek harmony with other men, without letting anyone trample on you." "And so," he says, "I try to light the way for the children. I try to help them understand the divine power that is in man — the

power to create, to destroy, the urge to fulfill himself, to account for
himself to that Supreme Force that seems to encompass us, to hold
the balance of the Universe, the force waiting for man to touch it to
liberate its hidden energies."[14]

Timi goes deeply into the meaning of exile and tries to come to
terms with his bitterness. While investigating the death of Naledi's
husband, he has been re-reading Richard Wright's *Uncle Tom's
Children* and wonders whether he too would continue to hate and
curse and burn with the same anger "and all those feelings that had
become reflexes among us blacks."[15] At first he feels that the solution lies in exile, but he has not reckoned with the all-encompassing
feeling of guilt which his departure from the scene of action
engenders, the longing "to be back in the fire, just so long as he
would be suffering along with others of his kind."[16] He also discovers, as we have seen, that the real Africa is not the concept of his
imagination. "No use in assuming an immediate common heritage
among Negroes everywhere. No use. You're an expatriate. Take your
chances, tread softly, human cultures have stone walls," Timi says.
Maybe, he continues, Africa has several enclaves with walls around
them and several crevices in the walls. "Take your chances. But what
are we seeking when we enter through the crevices? How can we be
sure? Maybe humanity must flow like water that cannot leave a
crevice unflooded. Woe unto those whose crevices are few, or who
don't have any."[17] There is hope, but it is qualified, and in any case
still lies in the future. Timi writes to Awoonor: "You see, once you
have left your native shores, you continue to circle up there, like a
bird in a storm. Only, the storm is inside yourself this time. When I
have thought things over, I may come back: but I suppose it must
always be on terms other than my own . . . ."[18]

The Wanderers is thus also the tragedy and the hope of Africa,
which Mphahlele has tried to symbolize in a story of his wanderings
and of the conflicts of those who will have to carry its heritage. Is this
too ambitious a task? The novel fails to become a convincing work of
art because the themes are illustrated by the story rather than arising
out of it. The work is often interesting, often poignant, but there is
little coherence. As a vehicle, the plot about the relationship
between Felang and his father begins far too late and is much too
slight, besides being insufficiently motivated. Timi and Felang are
both credible characters in that Mphahlele has been completely
honest and self-perceptive in presenting himself and his son to his
readers, but the story of their relationships is a trite one. Felang's

revolt, as a symbol for the struggle for self-identification of Africa's youth, would make sense only if it arose out of a specifically African situation, for instance, the boy's experiences in South Africa. But Felang's problems are the problems of adolescents of the last twenty years — of almost all colors, races, and provenance. The naiveté of Felang's parents in handling him, left without comment, leads one to believe that Mphahlele does not realize this. Thus the theme is based on false psychological premises.

This is not to say that the themes are presented inconsistently throughout. The personal search for a place in which a man can practice his simple human ideals is expressed in the intertwining lives of Timi and Steven — black and white — and in the death of Felang. The white man must break out of his cruel heritage, and the black man, for whom self-fulfillment at present lies only in exile and death, must bide his time. A will for survival — man must live — is no longer enough. Now Timi wants to "answer that longing to do something about something that nags everybody else,"[19] as he tells Awoonor when they discuss the Africanization of education. Endurance and the will to live are useless without an active attempt to control one's destiny. The role of embodying this quality of control is assigned to Naledi. She acquires it as a result of her suffering. Steven, after seeing her help the wounded during the riots, says: "A mysterious transformation had taken place in her. Her near-humble artlessness had gone. Her eyes bore the marks of suffering, but they were undaunted, even in a sad stoic manner . . . I knew at once that nobody, nothing was ever going to defile the quality of her endurance or break her will to live."[20] She is the only one at the end who comes to rest and has found her place. The others either continue to wander or have fallen by the wayside.

Mphahlele describes the novel as a personal account of search. One often wonders why he chose to present the work as fiction at all. Names of places and characters are sometimes changed, sometimes left intact. Thus we have Iboyoru for Nigeria and Lao-Kiku for Kenya, but the names of Zimbabwe and Namibia are not changed. If one is acquainted with the life story of Mphahlele and his circle, it becomes an amusing game to spot the real characters behind their pseudonyms. Don Peck of *Bongo* is Jim Bailey, owner of *Drum;* Steven Cartwright is Sylvester Stein, editor of *Bongo/Drum;* Tom Hobson is Tom Hopkinson, his successor; Lazy is Casey Motsisi, one of its journalist employees; Emil is probably Ulli Beier, and so forth. The names of some, again, are left unchanged, such as Awoonor, the writer. Mphahlele agreed, when asked, that *The Wanderers* is to a large extent autobiographical, but insists that it is more fiction than fact because it has a beginning and an ending, as distinct from *Down Second Avenue*. This, and probably the story of Naledi, are almost the only additions to an almost chronological account of Mphahlele's life. It starts where *Down Second Avenue* left off, with the departure for Nigeria. A brief summary of Timi's childhood as a herd-boy in the northern part of South Africa, his father's attack on his mother, and Timi's efforts and success in obtaining university degrees show that there is barely a pretense of fiction. One wonders a little how Mphahlele's oldest son, who remains a rebel, reacted to the slaying of his alter ego.

Timi's life in Nigeria and elsewhere finds verification in Mphahlele's essays. In "Travels of an Extramural Donkey,"[21] for instance, he describes his work as an extramural tutor in English literature on the staff of the University College of Ibadan in Northern Nigeria between 1959 and 1961. Sections of this account are identical with events in the novel. Other events, his loneliness and despair in London, for example, are verified by friends. "He could not survive in a condition of anonymity," Mphahlele says of Timi. "He seemed to feel a nonperson," an old South African friend, a prominent clergyman, says of Mphahlele when he appeared suddenly on the doorstep of his London home in the early hours of the morning.

The Wanderers is often so intensely personal as to give the impression of a revelation and a cleansing of the soul. The true events are not just the raw material for creative writing; they are raw indeed, undigested and unembellished. This section of his autobiographical writing deals with the most desperate period of his life. Homesick, ridden with guilt about his departure, unhappy in the lack of cooperation in his work, disillusioned with Africa, he seized his pen and put it all down on paper as he had done once before. But was it perhaps impossible for a man of his shy and retiring nature to reveal himself to this extent? He thus hid behind the thin shadow of Timi Tabane's identity. We see him standing back and watching himself in his first few months alone in exile. "Night after night, week after week, Timi walked from one end of town to another; he traced the arc the Marina makes along the waterfront, from one end to the other. Night after night the sea air beat against his face or caressed it; the water beat against the concrete wall just under his feet. . . ."[22]

This, then, may be the main reason why Mphahlele presents *The Wanderers* as a novel, and one of which he is possibly not aware. He insists that the work is fiction, that he intended it that way:

It has an autobiographical framework and it has real life people in it, but it is still more fiction than autobiography. I plotted it that way in the sense that I wanted to bring out the central character at different points. I then said to myself I want to find out in my own life what exile has led to. It has led to a disorientation in the children. It has led to a disorientation in my own self and it has led to discoveries in other territories and a realization of myself. Then I said I don't want to leave it as an open-ended thing in terms of a father-son relationship. Something has to happen to the son and that is a fictional plot. In that way I have a beginning and an ending, as distinct from *Down Second Avenue*. To that extent it is more fiction than autobiography.[23]

Mphahlele complains that people "keep wanting to judge by purely novelistic standards which are orthodox, forgetting that the novel form is most receptive to all kinds of materials. What you want to say defines its form," he says.[24] This may be so, but it does not prove that the ideal form has been chosen for definition. *Down Second Avenue* is the more powerful work, not because it has something more important to say, but because, by his own definition, Mphahlele chose a form that allowed him the right amount of freedom in which to say it.

What does Mphahlele himself demand in a novel? In *African Image* he says that novelists like Chinua Achebe, James Ngugi, and others succeed "according to the measure in which they get into their characters to reveal what they are like as individuals among people."[25] A novelist must dramatize conflict, he says, but he must also present characters who stand for more than themselves.

E. M. Forster, Mphahlele tells us, says of Dostoevsky's characters and situations that "infinity attends them."[26] The only instance in *The Wanderers* where any attempt is made to present such a character is Naledi. She is intended to grow in stature until she can endure infinitely and come to terms with her suffering. From a diffident country girl she turns into a sophisticated woman, sufficiently human and individual to disregard racial barriers and, unlike Timi, content to live and work on another continent. Unfortunately, she never comes to life. She is neither visible nor tangible like Mphahlele's women characters in his earlier fiction, who leave their canvas to move and talk and act.

Naledi remains two-dimensional; the terms used in describing her are stilted. Timi first sees her when her husband's friend, Diliza, brings her to his house.

While Karabo was busying herself in the cooking corner of our front room, I took the first opportunity to look closely at Naledi and make small talk with her.
    She was a pretty young woman. Quite thin, with doleful eyes. Her face was well chiselled. She had a strong mouth but smiled weakly and shyly.[27]

This is hardly promising as an introduction to a young woman who causes one white man of some prominence to fall in love with her and marry her, a policeman to try and commit rape, and even the timid Timi to fall into sexual temptation which he resists with some effort. It never becomes clear why these men are all attracted to her; we are simply asked to accept this. Timi spends many days with Naledi when they search for her husband, but although they talk endlessly, their discussions are only about her early life and we learn little about her as a person. Timi finds her "charming beyond words: a child of the night who was not meant to flourish in the rude naked light of day." When one night only his "inbred shyness," not "shame or loyalty to a wife or anything as lofty as that"[28] stops the desire storming inside him, the attraction still eludes the reader. The scene is introduced by Timi's thoughts about Naledi as a woman, but his metaphor is a most unfortunate choice by a man who is about to be almost overwhelmed with desire.

I did not think so much about her lost husband as her womanhood; her womanhood that lay fallow. I began wondering what she felt about it; what she felt about not having a man, not just as protection and main support but for the welfare of her body. Could a woman of twenty-nine simply close up, like a disused piece of land which could at any time open up to the sun and rain and air when one ploughed it? Did she require a period of regeneration or relearning before she could respond fully to a man's plough as it were?[29]

Steven also fails to communicate Naledi's essential qualities to the reader when he takes over as narrator. In his dreams and sexual fantasies he confuses the face of the black nanny of babyhood with his present servant, and with the young woman he now desires. He indicates that he is attracted to black women mainly because it is forbidden, almost as if it were a mere sexual aberration. Yet Naledi is the woman he eventually marries and casually expects his middle-class parents to accept. There is even less motivation for Naledi's acceptance of Steven as lover or husband. Nowhere in the section of the book dealing with their relationship is there any indication that Naledi cares for Steven. She certainly has little cause to do so. He treats her with condescension and she politely, and with some dignity, repulses this importunate white man. When he procures a domestic job for Naledi at her request, the following conversation ensues:

"You'll like it at Monty's. He's a good friend of mine. He laughs very loud. And Myrtle his wife is really fine."
"Thank you, Mr. Cartwright."
"And he'll pay you extra for your domestic science training."
"I'm grateful to you, Mr. Cartwright."[30]

Not long afterwards, when Steven visits her in her kitchen, he tells her he is "madly" fond of her. The love scenes between this weakly defined couple are almost incredibly clumsy. It is not as though Mphahlele is incapable of writing emotively or delicately about love. He does so with some skill when he describes Timi's and Karabo's sexual relationship. Timi is unhappy when Karabo rejects him and wonders why she cannot sustain periods of sexual intensity to match his own. Especially during the time of the harmattan in Iboyoru he is like an animal in heat. But he knows his deep love for her, and thus, instead of inflicting himself on her, he drives like a madman on the Great North Road, going into the thick of the harmattan. Many a night "he would, if repulsed, go out on the veranda, panting and yearning and burning to find release for his energy."[31] When the air had tempered him he would return to bed. Whenever Karabo went to the door to look at him sitting on the step and asked, "What's the matter?" he would say "Nothing." There is no hint of any remotely similar emotions of affection and solicitude, or any other form of genuine love, between Steven and Naledi.

As a portrayal of a strong-willed, maturing girl of charm and grace, Naledi, in spite of her superior education, stands a long way behind Karabo in "Mrs. Plum"; Pinkie, the Coffee-Cart Girl; or Diketso in the Lesane stories. Karabo in *The Wanderers*, on the other hand, comes through in successive glimpses that make up a convincing whole. She is patient and loyal in following her husband to the corners of the world because she never questions her function as a traditional African wife. When it comes to others, however, she is capable of spirited and determined action. Not many black women

in South Africa will argue with a white man, but Karabo refuses to
take nonsense from anyone. When a Greek cafe owner insists that
she and her child drink their soda outside in the street, she has the
last word in the argument that follows:

"Get out and drink outside!" the Greek shouted.
"I'm not going to drink outside. I paid for this lemonade."
"I say out, kaffir woman' "
"I'm not, Greek bastard! Carry me out if you want."
The Greek moves towards her.
"Just you touch me and you'll see your mother."
"Do you want me to call the police?"
"Shit. Bring back my money."
"The bottles are open already."
"There's your piss then! Now bring back my money and I'll go. Otherwise
call the police!"
"Here's your money!"
"I'm marking this shop, you hear me? When we begin to fight I'm coming
straight here to slit your throat. Look at my face and remember it! Come
let's go, Felang!"

When she tells Timi about it, she remarks dryly: "I don't know what
the boy made of it."[32]

Karabo provides some of the most picturesque language in the
novel, drawing on a mixture of vernacular proverbs and modern
colloquial images. She comes home after visiting a colleague of
Timi's, who had often been entertained by them. "You can't believe
it, Timi," she reports. "We ate rice and milk. We had meat only
once since we arrived — the first day. Mean people — ah! I hate
mean people. What's food but decayed stuff in the teeth, as our people say. And the man carries such a large tripe in his belly. The next
time he comes here, Timi, he's not going to touch this record player.
I can feel *Carmen Jones* crawl up to my gullet right now."[33]

She describes another acquaintance as having buttocks like the
backside of a Ford mustang car. When Timi and Karabo take some
friends to a nightclub, and the doorkeeper will not let one of the men
enter because he is not wearing a tie, it is Karabo who demands to
see the manager and tells him that he had better reconsider. "Why
all the fuss about ties anyhow?" she asks. "We didn't go about
dangling rags round our necks before you whites came to Africa."[34]
The manager apologizes and allows them to enter.

Karabo does not share Timi's guilt feelings about employing a servant in Iboyoru. The impudent Hassan, and the high-flown idiom in

which he speaks, makes her "quiver all over with impatience." She tells Timi that Hassan is so proud, "sometimes I just want to stand in the middle of the yard there and urinate."[35] Which, we are told, is exactly what Hassan did one morning, prior to his departure from their service. Timi, too, often encounters his wife's temperamental outbursts, and they leave him puzzled. If he makes her angry, she retires to one of the children's beds. Karabo speaks when she has something to say, even if she has to wake her husband in the middle of the night to say it, and then says what she means.

Mphahlele does not tell us much about his own wife in his autobiographical writing. It is clear, however, that someone who supported him in all his wanderings, who stood by his side in adversity and success, who carried eight children of whom four survived, and who, in one of their last ports of call, managed to study and acquire a new profession herself, must be a woman of the same stamina, courage, and forthrightness that he successfully depicts in Karabo.

The different ways in which Karabo and Timi handle Felang is characteristic. It is Karabo whom he exasperates most, often to the point of hysteria, partly because Timi leaves most of the child rearing to her, and partly because the psychological nuances of the generation gap are beyond her comprehension. Since Karabo has never been at a loss to communicate, Felang's silences are inexplicable to her. She can only counter them with a frantic: "What's *eating* the boy?"

Timi, on the other hand, senses the boy's feelings instinctively, but finds him difficult to understand for other reasons. He cannot grasp why Felang quarrels with privilege, when he himself was almost defeated by the sheer effort to survive. He is far more anxious to understand and help Felang than is Karabo. When he expresses an interest in drama Karabo exclaims "Theater my foot!" but Timi arranges for him to go on a trip with a friend, who would be able to help him gain a theater scholarship. When Felang proves that he is not really serious in his ambition, Timi, still patient, merely asks him what his problem is. There is no problem, Felang insists. Timi is painfully aware of the boy's struggles and despair, but his efforts to help him are in vain.

It is not just Timi who fails to understand Felang but Mphahlele himself as the author. He attempts to put down on paper a portrait of his own son, without, in actual fact, having succeeded in bridging the gap between them. Felang's sullenness, his silences, his evasions, his bids for attention, and his bravado are the hallmarks of the modern teen-ager in fiction and real life. It is not his blackness, but the malady of his generation that motivates him.

Timi's life story, actions, dialogue, and thoughts are so close to Mphahlele's own that it is impossible to consider him as a separate character in a novel. Whether we hear him as narrator himself or of him in the third person as told by Steven or the author, he remains the voice of Mphahlele. Yet Mphahlele is capable of standing back and seeing himself objectively, as others would see him. By nature Timi is gentle, shy, and scholarly and has to prod himself into action when it becomes necessary. Karabo tells Naledi about their courtship: "He was so shy when we first met I've always wondered where he got the courage to say he loved me. When we were courting, he'd sit for hours without saying anything, especially when my mother was in. He'd just sit there like a mountain and say nothing, and just drink one cup of tea after another."[36]

He confesses his lack of control over his children and tells how he would rehearse in his mind what he was about to say to them. Timi, like Mphahlele, is deeply compassionate, and thus never ceases in his efforts to understand his eldest son. Felang's actions and ideals, like those of the black students Mphahlele encountered in the States, seemed to contradict everything in which he, Timi, believed. Only in Felang's death do their ideals meet. Timi realizes that the basic truths he teaches are limited at present by the cruelty of the times. But his grief for his son is alleviated by hope. "Aren't we happier when our love activates things in people than when it founders on passive ground?" he asks Steven.[37] He says this at the beginning of the book, but it is a conclusion he draws from the end event, Felang's death. It answers, perhaps, a question Timi asks at the beginning of events, about his life among slum dwellers: "Why did one's efforts to concern oneself with other people's miseries seem so utterly futile in relation to what was to be done?"[38] The answer lies in the continuous hope of activity promoting better things, a dream which can only come true through love and compassion. This can be described as the aim of Timi/Mphahlele's existence.

The novel contains a horde of minor characters who are introduced mainly as background. There are Timi's neighbors in Nadia Street, who, so many years after the *Drum* stories, have receded into the shadows. The incidents, though often amusing, stand isolated and no longer combine to create an authentic and vivid atmosphere. Events are described instead of being dramatically presented. When he talks about the township on a Saturday night, we are told what we *might* see and *would* hear. In his earlier writing we were able to see and hear it happening ourselves. Mphahlele is a victim of what he calls the tyranny of place, the need for constant contact with a locale, with its smell, its taste, and texture. Without this contact he cannot reproduce the scenes so that they come alive for the reader. Speaking about the Nigerian and Kenyan sections of the novel, Mphahlele admits that one does not get this sense of place. "I do describe Lagos and so on, but I don't dwell long enough on the landscape and on the physical setting."[39]

Also appearing on the canvas are Timi's colleagues on *Bongo*, who give Mphahlele an opportunity for some lively sketches. Then there are his new friends and colleagues in exile, the servants, the petty criminals. He pays tribute to a real character whom he admires, Kofi Awoonor. In the early section Diniza, a medical man who introduces Naledi to Timi and Steven, appears frequently. He is purely functional, however, as the revolutionary who is consumed with hatred of the white man, and is thus contrasted with Timi and Naledi who come to terms with their bitterness.

Steven Cartwright is Mphahlele's first attempt at a sympathetic portrait of a white man. However, like Timi, he lacks perspective as a fictitious character. He, too, is Mphahlele's voice as narrator. The main difference between Timi and Steven — and at the same time their similarity — is the emphasis they put on their color. Mphahlele is still under the illusion that the white man in South Africa is as conscious of being white as the black man is of being black. A man like Steven would certainly have strong feelings of racial guilt, but they would not consume him in the same way as the black man is consumed in exile. The attempt to motivate Steven's love for Naledi, as we have seen, is psychologically naive.

There is an amusing pen portrait of Steven's mother and father whose dialogue provides comic relief. The father is described as "a retired mathematics professor walking about with a pipe-smoking detachment as if life were an eternal maze of angles and triangles and quadrilaterals and trapeziums and circles and tangents."

"Why are you sitting on a broken chair, Felix, naughty boy?" his wife asks him.

"All the other chairs are occupied, dear."

"Why don't you take mine, Felix?"

"You're sitting on it, dear."
"Funny man, your father, Steven. . . ."[40]

However, though the mother is shown to be domineering, the
character of the parents does not help to explain Steven's actions.
The parents seem to accept his marriage across the color line with an
equanimity quite unheard of among their class of white South
African.

In the police sergeant who quells the riots, and the constable who
attacks Naledi, Mphahlele goes back to the white stock-characters of
black South African fiction, who talk with their guns and their sex
organs. There is some attempt to make the constable plausible as a
human being, by making him the child of a German missionary who
shot his wife, set their house on fire, and then killed himself. The
sergeant merely blusters.

The Wanderers includes one or two successful portraits of real
people, such as the fascinating, mysterious, and paradoxical owner of
Drum/Bongo, who appears as Don Peck. He is wealthy, but refuses
his staff deserved raises in salary with a smile, and picks his
charitable actions carefully. Cynically, he denies that he is interested
in anything other than in making money — "this is a picture
magazine and not a political propaganda sheet," he complains[41] —
yet he fearlessly agrees to publish anti-government exposés. He
remains behind the scenes, and though he never lists orders or gives
them in a formal manner, "he brings them in during a discussion;
you can't mistake them for suggestions." His eyes, Steven says, tell
you that it would be folly to do so.[42] Then there is an interesting portrait of Emil, an Austrian who has totally integrated into African
society in the north of Iboyoru. He did not identify in any clumsy or
neurotic way. "He simply made friendships among those of his class
among black and white without imposing himself on the indigenous
people like one who might think he was doing them a favor," we are
told. He is basically humble, with a shy smile, and never rushed into
things. "But he always knew where to come in, and then he threw
himself into the work with resolve while some of the expatriates
jeered and scoffed on the sidelines."[43]

These are the characters that people the strife-torn subcontinent
of Mphahlele's novel. They are held together tenuously by their
association with Timi in his wanderings. They, and the events in
which they feature, are seen through the eyes of three narrators,
presumably to give three different points of view. There is little
difference, however, in the tone of narration, or in the attitude of the

narrators toward the events and problems that are described and discussed. In fact, it is difficult for the reader to remember that it is not Timi talking throughout. No perspective is gained and the tone remains flat. The technique thus appears merely contrived, especially the section narrated by Steven, whose thoughts are intentionally confused because he is making notes on recent events during an illness. "In between drugs I want to jot down some notes," he says.[44]

The constant shifts in time and place destroy the continuity and hamper what little action there is in the novel. Mphahlele seems to have lost his skill in stirring up a lively interest in the episodes of his life. Most of the time nothing happens, and when it does, we often know about it only through hearsay. Timi is in an African country during the overthrow of a dictator, but the reader learns of it only through endless and dull political discussions. There is a singular lack of excitement about events that promise to be dramatic. We hear little about Timi's escape from South Africa, for instance, even though his journey must have been as full of adventure as Alfred Hutchinson's in his autobiographical *Road to Ghana*[45] and that of the fictitious Makhaya in Bessie Head's novel, *When Rain Clouds Gather*.[46] The picaresque simply does not interest Mphahlele.

Neither the story of Naledi's search for her husband nor the account of the mobs protesting against the carrying of passes by women have the terseness of Mphahlele's reports for *Drum* on which they are based. We see the rioting villages and the brutal police, who move in Saracen tanks, through the eyes of Steven, who exchanges stilted comments with a white priest. The mingling of fact and fiction enables us neither to identify with the passion of the characters as we would in an imaginary story, nor to share in the urgent indignation of a successful journalistic exposé. A side-plot concerns a white friend of Steven's, Barney, whose wife leaves him for the black Diniza. We hear of her departure in an almost casual telephone conversation between Barney and Steven. Two pages later, in another fleeting telephone call, Barney announces that she is back again.

"Hallo, Steve!"

"Hallo, Barney! What's new?"

"Well, what do you know? Joan has come back. Last night as we were talking on your terrace, who'd have thought it would happen today — so bloody gloomy things looked then."

"How's she, Barney? I mean what does she feel about it all?"

"Just said, 'I'm sorry, Barney, it didn't work after all. I don't know what

came over me.' Maybe your theory's right Steve."
    "What theory? I've a waggonload of them."
    "That it was Diliza's act of revenging himself against us — all whites. By
the way, I dropped by to see Karabo. . . ."[47]

The story of the rape attempt on Naledi reaches the reader
thirdhand. We learn of it in a conversation between Steven and a
woman lawyer, Anda Kaplan. Naledi, it appears, gave the lawyer a
detailed account of events, including the actual words used by the
protagonists. Steven, still making notes while on his sick bed, writes
down what Anda Kaplan tells him that Naledi told her. A more
circuitous method of reporting dramatic happenings is difficult to
imagine.
    The only events that seem to happen before our eyes are those
concerning Felang. We see him arguing with his parents, misbehav-
ing at school and at home, running away and returning. Although
Timi as narrator tells us about it, the anguish of the three people
concerned makes it real and immediate.
    The general effect of *The Wanderers* is one of lack of movement.
It is far more static than Mphahlele's earlier fiction. In a description
of a party in East Africa, for example; people "stand and talk,"
"say," "continue," "hail," "remark," "leave," "come in," "comment," "explain," "look at each other." The only other verb used in
this passage describes lights as glittering. Again, almost only in the
scenes with Felang — and with Karabo — does the language come
alive. Felang cannot be still. He refuses to answer questions about
himself. There is no problem, he assures his father. But as he stands
there silently, "he beat his fist into the palm of his other hand a few
times, as if to use the action to say what he could not or dared not articulate."[48] The style rouses itself a little before that, to give a vivid
description of one of the frequent drinking parties held by *Bongo*
staff. Timi's colleagues celebrate at the home of one of their number.
The refrigerator, the classical music, the quotations from
Shakespeare, and the sophisticated wisecracks are displayed against
the background of a segregated slum. Mphahlele was never really
part of this scene, but he handles it skillfully in that he motivates the
drunken frenzy of these parties as "pressure . . . from deep inside for
something to break loose so the tensions dissolve or spill out into the
next morning."[49]
    The story of Naledi's search for her husband is too drawn out, but
the end of the quest is presented effectively as a climax. The ultimate irony of the success of their search and its uselessness, the

silent communion of the widow when she discovers that Rampa is dead, and the ritual observed suggest a scene from a Becket play.

The love scenes, on the other hand, are inhibited and devoid of tension. It is impossible to sympathize or even feel much interest in the relationship between Steven and Naledi, as we are told so little about their real feelings. Thus, apart from a few scenes, the limited range of emotions keeps the novel on an even, low key.

The Wanderers procured for Mphahlele the degree of Doctor of Philosophy from the University of Denver in June, 1968. An extract appeared in *African Arts/Arts d'Afrique* prior to publication.[50] Reviews like John Povey's in *African Studies Review*[51] and Barney C. McCartney's in *East Africa Journal*[52] are typical in that they criticize the lack of controlling organization and the contrived form of narration. Thus, what has been said in the present analysis is substantiated by other critical appraisals.

CHAPTER 8

A Bright New Day

IN June, 1974, Mphahlele became a full professor of the University of Pennsylvania. He lives in Philadelphia in suburban surroundings, as he did in Denver, chafing against his bourgeois, academic existence. In "Tyranny of Place" he tells us how, when he bought a house in Denver, he smashed up a piano which the previous owner had left in the basement, because he resented being drawn into a piano-ornamented culture.

He continues, however, to do what he enjoys most, teaching English literature. And of course he has not stopped writing. He completed a new novel some time ago, but it is still awaiting publication. "Kwacha! A Bright New Day" was its original title. Later he changed it to "The House of Chirundu," and at the time of writing the manuscript is entitled "Chirundu."

In order to complete a study of Mphahlele's writing up to the present time, it is essential to consider this novel, even though it is still in manuscript form. We need to know in what direction Mphahlele's writing is pointing and to investigate why it has not found a publisher as readily as his earlier works.

The action takes place in the 1960's in Zambia, although the country is never named. By placing the action beyond the border of South Africa, Mphahlele is moving into the mainstream of African literature. *The Wanderers* takes place outside South Africa to a large extent, but always as seen from a South African point of view.

In critical works on African writing and in anthologies today, South African fiction is too often omitted. White fiction writers are considered as too remote from the African mainstream; and black South African writers of fiction, producing in exile, such as Alex La Guma and Mphahlele himself, are unaccountably ignored. By writing a novel freed of purely local problems and personal contingencies, Mphahlele could bridge the gap between South African fiction and African continental literature.

158

"Chirundu" is the story of the fall from power of a political figure, Chimba Chirundu, and of the dissolution of his marriage. Mphahlele professes to explore the dynamics of power in relation to domestic life, marital relations, the African's attitude toward polygamy, and the modern woman's rejection of it. At the same time it is a study of African independence and its effect of hope and disillusionment on several people bound together by circumstances or relationships.

When the story begins, Chirundu has already fallen from grace. As a Cabinet Minister, he has been demoted from the Portfolio of Interior Affairs to Transport and Public Works, and his wife Tirenje has brought a charge of bigamy against him. While still Minister of the Interior, he had ordered the detention, as possible spies, of about a dozen political refugees from South Africa, Rhodesia, Angola, and other countries — all those who did not fall under a particular refugee organization.

The novel opens with a conversation between two of these prisoners, Pitso, a black South African, and Chieza from Rhodesia. The prison warden remonstrates with Pitso for screaming in his sleep and ends his diatribe about their ingratitude, when after all they have been given refuge in this country, with the words he always uses as he wakes them: "*Kwatcha*, wake up, it's a bright new day." Pitso and Chieza jeer at him. They have been in prison for twenty-seven months. They discuss their lot and then turn to the newspaper which a South African friend, "Studs" Letanka, has sent them. In it there is news of the impending bigamy lawsuit brought against the Minister who caused their detention. The second woman in the case, they read with interest, is one Monde.

Chirundu, we learn later, comes from Shimoni, a district in the northeast of the unnamed country. His father converted to Christianity when Chimba was six years old and subsequently changed from a sensible though obstinate man to one obsessed by religion and a household tyrant. His two wives leave him. Chimba Chirundu teaches at a mission school of the Seventh Day Adventist Church but is disgusted by the hypocrisy of its leaders, and especially of the superintendent. He has an affair with a senior pupil, Tirenje Mirimba, and she becomes pregnant. The superintendent asks him to resign, although by then Tirenje had already left school. The interview leads to an outburst from Chirundu against the hypocrisy of the churches in Africa. He resigns, and leaves teaching for politics as a member of the National Alliance Party.

Chimba and Tirenje are married, first under Bemba traditional law, and then under a British colonial ordinance that specifically prohibits polygamy. Tirenje insists on this, making it quite clear that she is not prepared to share him with another woman. The couple move to the Copperbelt, where Chirundu continues his political activities enthusiastically. Even before independence he is aware of the realities of politics; for instance, that one cannot plug higher wages for mine workers for propaganda purposes when an independent African government, which would have to deal with economic problems, is imminent. The leader of the party has great faith in Chirundu, making him leader of the youth movement and paying him a good salary.

The first sign of friction in Chirundu's marriage comes when Tirenje asks to help in his political work and he tells her that he needs a woman to be at his service at home. Tirenje also feels that he is neglecting her in bed. When she confronts him with this, he takes her ferociously, "like a python," as she used to say when they first made love. By this time, however, he has met Monde in the capital where his work often takes him. Monde is an administrative secretary in the Ministry of Commerce and Industry. Self-possessed and sophisticated, she has been trained as a secretary in England and has always lived in the city. Chirundu makes her his mistress. Her attitude is a very matter-of-fact one. When Chirundu asks her, "Would you rather take a man who can give you security as a legal husband?" she replies: "It does not matter at present. When I want such a man I will tell you. And if you don't want to be that man, you will tell me."[1]

Independence comes, and life seems perfect for Chirundu. "*Kwacha!* A new bright day had dawned. October 1964. I stood on the hill to see it come. Grandfather was so right. I felt so big."[2] He moves to the capital, promising to fetch his family when he is settled. Months pass, and he continues to stall although he visits them often. He is happy in his relationship with both women and would like to continue in this way.

Two years after the declaration of independence his fortune begins to change. In a cabinet reshuffle he is made Minister of Transport and Public Works. He fears that the President has found him too tough in the more responsible department, and tries to see his demotion as an impetus in his efforts to fulfill his destiny; he is sure that he is meant for greater things. In the same year his nephew Moyo, son of his deceased half-sister, arrives in the city with Moyo's grandfather. At his request, Chirundu provides his nephew with work in the transport section. Moyo attends night classes run by an international organization and is especially enthusiastic about lessons in the history of the labor movement, taught by the South African lecturer Letanka, a former brilliant mathematician. At length he becomes involved in labor union activities, much to his uncle's distress.

Chirundu decides to build a house of his own, rather than rely on an official residence, and when it is completed he moves in with Monde. He visits his family less and less frequently, and Tirenje and the children finally go to live with her father. Chirundu visits her there, and with great dignity she pleads with him to take her back with him to the city, although she knows that he has another woman there. Impulsively he tells her to pack.

Moyo now emerges as the man of whom Chirundu must beware. It is he who puts up his aunt Tirenje, with her children, rather than let her stay in a hotel until Chirundu can procure an apartment for them; who arranges for the two women to meet and tells his uncle with barely concealed satisfaction how they had to be kept apart by the gardener. Chirundu can no longer deal with his problems or even face them: he does not ask either of the women about the incident. His reaction to a letter his wife writes to him — a plea from the heart, asking him what she must do and begging him to discuss the situation sensibly — is to mutter complaints about why she had to spoil the whole thing. Tirenje has too much pride to put up with the situation; she first returns to her father, then decides to go to the Copperbelt and find work there. She is expecting another child which she subsequently loses.

Chirundu realizes that he should ask Tirenje for a divorce, but he still does not want to lose her or the children. On the other hand, he has no intention of giving up Monde. People are beginning to talk. The President sets him an ultimatum, either divorce his wife or get rid of his mistress. Driven into a corner, his "house" crumbling, in defiance and anger, he takes Monde to a marriage officer. The officer makes Chirundu swear that he married the first time by Bemba law and that his second marriage therefore annuls the first one. This is quite correct, but he says nothing to the officer or to Monde about the registration of his first marriage under the colonial ordinance. Later he claims that his purpose was to fight a system. "The [colonial] Ordinance should recognize traditional marriage as something that cannot be superseded, because we are polygamous," he says.[3] His lawyer tells him that one cannot test a law by breaking it; rather, one should try and change it by parliamentry procedure. Chirundu of course knows this full well. He admits to himself that he was swept off his feet by Monde, but he still feels that he is in love with Tirenje. His indignation at being forced to make a choice is quite genuine.

When he hears that Tirenje has laid a charge of bigamy against him, he first thinks that Moyo or the prosecutor — an enemy of long standing — must have put her up to it, but then realizes that she is quite capable of making such a move herself. Tirenje later says that she merely wanted to force Chirundu to return to her, preferably without a political portfolio.

Chirundu, in his anger and feelings of guilt, now expedites his downfall in every direction. He causes government drivers to be dismissed for keeping official vehicles out after hours, although he knows that some of them are doing so at the instigation of the officials who are using them. This turns both the officials and the transport workers' union against him. In the cabinet he openly refers to scandals concerning cabinet ministers which have been hushed up.

The court case has been proceeding throughout the narration of these events. While it is already well under way, Tirenje's companion, an elderly relative, brings Chirundu to the house for a discussion, but there is little left for them to say. Both realize that the rift is final. Chirundu is found guilty of bigamy and sentenced to one year's imprisonment without the option of a fine. He meets his sentence stony-faced, thinking that the time will come when the British judge who sentences him will no longer function in an African land and he, Chirundu, will be in a position to deal with the prosecutor, this fat creature, educated and modelled in the British image. Tirenje breaks down at the end of the trial and screams for her man to come back to her. She is escorted from the court room.

The trial appears to be the signal for a breakdown of law and order in the land. Not only is Chirundu's house burnt down — at first figuratively in Tirenje's words — but the whole city is ablaze. Suspected Portuguese spies, who crossed the border a month after the Portuguese had bombed villages in Chirundu's country, are acquitted by a white judge who reverses a black magistrate's verdict on appeal. The youth brigade of the ruling party, encouraged by the minister in charge of them and by the President, marches on the court building to protest. The trade union of the transport workers, of which Moyo is a member, comes out on strike. The youth brigade march to the university where they are joined by students, also picking up the strikers along the way. Together they march to the prison to lynch the Portuguese prisoners. After a set-to, the police succeed in turning them away. They then pull a wagon full of human dung to the President's residence and tip it out on the lawn. Transport House is ablaze; Chimba's new house, too, is burnt down, and the old gardener, the only one left there, sees Tirenje at the gate and hears her say that it is finished. He tells this to Moyo, at the same time making it clear that he would deny it if officially questioned.

After these outbursts, things quiet down. The President in a broadcast asks the strikers either to return to work or be dismissed and promises further negotiations. The university is to close down and students must reapply to enter.

The South African prisoner, Pitso, decides to return to his own country at the risk of imprisonment and maltreatment there. Studs Letanka dies as the result of a car accident. Moyo's grandfather, too, is dead. Moyo is expecting his sister in the city to enroll in a school of nursing. He visits the Rhodesian prisoner Chieza in jail, but he is afraid to visit Chirundu while he is there. "I don't know what I feel," he says to Chieza,

"Yes — er — I think I *am* afraid somewhat. It's the kind of fear — I think — you know when you've got a killer of an animal in a cage — you know it can't break out — but you go and touch the wall of the cage — and something — something seems to tug at your nerves — you tremble ever so little — the slightest movement in the cage makes you jump or jerk or anything—."

Chieza is more afraid that Chirundu will come back one day "fighting, maybe meaner than ever before."[4]

We expect a writer of Mphahlele's standing to turn to a novel again after an interval of five years only if he has something important to communicate, not merely to entertain. Yet at a first reading "Chirundu" seems almost trivial. It begins by introducing a cabinet minister as having committed a crime so petty that even his prisoners are contemptuous. The prisoners feel, however, that there must be something behind it, and it seems obvious that Mphahlele intended something deeper in the novel than the chicaneries of the vain, power-hungry, male-chauvinistic character of the title.

"Chirundu," it would appear, is a dirge for Africa, where anguished disillusionment is the keynote. Hope for a bright new day is dim indeed. At the beginning of the novel "*kwacha*" is the unreasoning faith of the simple-minded prison warden; at the end the losing battle against forces that destroy the hope of Africa is dismissed with a shrug. In *The Wanderers* the South African characters were searching for a better life. Here, in Zambia, with the arrival of independence, people thought that they had found it, but expectation turned to disillusionment and bitterness.

The note of disillusionment is set from the beginning. The two prisoners, Pitso and Chieza, joke with each other, but their main interest and subject of conversation are Pitso's bowel movements. Pitso, whose nights are full of terror, wants to go back to South Africa. He has crossed the border to freedom, but finds himself detained. He sums up his disappointment in the new dawn: "To get your ass shot up in action's much more dignified than developing piles just sitting on your ass here living through the fuckin' kwacha routine with that halfwit."[5] Studs Letanka, another South African, has also been disillusioned. A brilliant mathematician, he left his country because he could not stand the social snobbery at the Black University at which he taught but found no worthwhile opening for a black man elsewhere. He turns to history and comes to Zambia to teach adults, leaving his wife in England. He drinks too much, and dies as the result of a car crash. The Zambians themselves have not found independence the heady medicine they expected. The government is often incompetent, as in its handling of the political refugee problem — more often still, corrupt. A rape charge against a minister is never brought to court and the victim deported; a minister wishes to divest himself of his Afro-American wife and has a colleague deport her. Democracy and socialism are suspended when expedient. At best, there is smug paternalism, not even real independence; colonialism continues in many aspects, such as the court system, depending as it does on British custom and being influenced by British judges.

But all is not gloom: there *is* a glimmer on the horizon, and for the new generation, exemplified by Moyo, there might yet be a bright new day. *His* house has not burnt down; on the contrary, it has yet to be built. And its foundation will be solid, for unlike Chirundu, he has not lost touch with real tradition. His faith in the power of continuity, as exemplified by the ancestors, is strong. "I've got Ambuye (his grandfather)," he says with confidence, after the old man's death. He describes the events after the trial: "The terror of it shook me up so bad that I was left wondering what kind of animal we created when we shout and boo and dance and shriek and elect people and never get to know how government works, even while we are forming it, let alone afterwards."

By calling the novel "Chirundu," Mphahlele emphasizes the character rather than the theme. It might be better to revert to one of the earlier titles, the sardonic "Bright New Day," or the symbolic "House of Chirundu," since the portrayal of the title character is not a happy one. Chimba Chirundu embodies the African politician at the dawn of the independence era. The idealism — the fight for independence and social democracy — is already taken for granted and the practical aspect is emphasized. Chirundu lives in the present. He rejects Christianity along with all European ideas that had been dumped on Africa, as he puts it, but he believes in traditionalism only if it serves a purpose, or as individual choice, never as a stance. He is motivated entirely by a thirst for power, politically, personally, and sexually. Power to him is an area in which he can express himself. He loves it for its own sake and appears confident in his "profession."

Chirundu is tall and there is something aristocratic about his appearance. His clothes are always of the best, chosen with care even when he appears in court. During his trial he looks bored and resentful. Weakness in others he professes to find irritating.

But is he really as cool and confident as he appears? He continually has to remind himself that he is destined for greatness. "I'm a big man, a responsible man, a public servant."[7] He must assure himself over and over again that he is right, that he has no need to feel guilty for having two women, for are Africans not traditionally polygamous? Then why is he afraid to tell Tirenje the truth? And why will he not divorce her or separate from Monde if doing neither means the ruin of the career which is so important to him? The answer is that he needs the reassurance of another woman in love with him, for he suspects that Tirenje is the stronger partner in the marriage, and this he cannot tolerate. He speaks contemptuously of Moyo, but what upsets him is that his nephew discovers him to be vulnerable in his public life, just as Tirenje does in the domestic sphere.

Chirundu is a man filled with hate and guilt. In his childhood he saw his father disintegrate after conversion to Christianity. "Now there was an alien fire in him," Chirundu recalls, "and yet it seemed to torture him even while he bandied Bible and hymn book everywhere. He laid down restrictions. He commanded us to pray morning and night, go to three church services every Sunday."[8] The father abandons one wife while the other, Chimba's mother, later leaves him. Chimba makes his own way in life by clinging tenaciously to his grandfather's prediction that he was meant for great things. Chimba is told that after he was born his grandfather held him in his arms and said: "This boy shall bear my name Chimba. He shall walk straight as a bluegum tree and yield no ground to anyone but his king. I can see him standing on that hill there against the growing light of a new dawn. And he will tell the people to wake up for a new day has come. . . ."[9] Even after his downfall, when he has nothing left but his determination and faith in himself, he feels sure that he will make a come-back. We are reminded of Zungu in "Man Must Live." Has Mphahlele then come full circle, abandoning his search and his wanderings to conclude that all man can do is cling tenaciously to his faith in life and his destiny? This would be understandable, since Mphahlele is still in exile, displaced, with hope of a return to the country of his destiny as remote as ever.

If, however, we are being asked to admire Chirundu for this quality, then the character sketch is an abject failure. Chirundu is totally unsympathetic and repulsive. He is introduced in the novel as so contemptible to his enemies, the refugees he has imprisoned, that they cannot even hate him. Little follows to change this first impression. He rejects Christianity because of the enslaving institutions to which it gave rise, but does not accept faith in the ancestors, an alternative that would also have provided him with the sense of humility that his father had found wanting in him.

In love he is insensitive, callous, and entirely selfish. He tells the superintendent of the church school that he will not be pushed into marrying Tirenje (after he has made her pregnant) just to satisfy the church's scruples, but he does not seem to have considered the girl's feelings in the matter. He ignores the feelings of the two women entirely, and acts in the matter of his two marriages purely for his own purposes. Sometimes he feels guilt, but never real remorse.

Intelligent, capable, and ruthless, he has no difficulty in achieving his ambitions in love and in his career. "I always felt the drive to achieve something and simply took for granted that I was going to own it," he says.[10] In this instance he is speaking of his conquest of Monde. He reaches a cabinet post in the same way. He is not as adroit as he imagines, however. He underestimates both Tirenje and Moyo, he performs his functions as Minister of the Interior with unnecessary harshness, and he antagonizes colleagues and officials who could be useful to him. We gather that the rest of the Cabinet finds him a convenient scapegoat for the press when there is criticism.

Unpleasant as he is, Chirundu comes to life to a greater extent than the other characters. They are mainly assigned characteristics that will complete various aspects of the picture Mphahlele wishes to present. About Monde, for instance, we learn little other than that she is sophisticated, socially adept, and very sexy. It is mainly her external characteristics that are described. Studs Letanka says that he does not know what to make of her and neither, really, does the author. It is sufficient to indicate that she is seductive, but sophisticated enough to make herself less dispensable than a common concubine. Moyo's grandfather stands for the wisdom of old age; Chieza, the Rhodesian, and Pitso, the South African, perform the function of a chorus. Studs Letanka is more interesting and, one feels, a tribute being paid to a real character whom Mphahlele admired.

Moyo represents the hope of a new dawn. By his youth, innocence, and idealism, he serves both as a contrast to Chirundu and as his nemesis. There is some attempt to define him as a character in his own right, but it is a little forced. He was a mischievous child who liked to play pranks and laughed easily. He matures into a young man of responsibility and sensitivity. There is a strong bond between him and Tirenje.

In Tirenje we have again one of Mphahlele's forceful women, but at the same time she represents Africa. Her physical characteristics are significant. She is firmly built, with strong legs and a well-rounded bosom. She walks like a woman who knows where she is going. Her voice has an earthy tone and her steady eyes look you straight in the face, unlike Monde's which cannot hold their gaze long. Thus she is described variously by her husband, Moyo, and Studs Letanka. In her youth she was shy but never timid. She is submissive to her man to an extent — she likes him to hold her like a python — but she will not share him, and fights fiercely for her rights. She has real love for her husband, though sometimes she wonders to what extent she fears him and is overpowered by him. Above all, she is chaste — she resists temptation even after Chimba has deserted her — loyal, and true.

Tirenje is not merely a home-maker. She wants to work side by side with her husband and is prepared to support herself when he leaves her. Tirenje is not a symbol for tradition as opposed to modern ways; she is Africa not of the past but of the present and the future, modern in outlook but with a firm basis of traditionalism. More than

anything else she has great dignity which never leaves her, even in
her confrontation with her rival when they almost come to blows,
and when she pleads with her husband for her rights. This is her
strength, as Chimba well understands. "Tirenje never raised her
voice," he says, "even when she felt passionately about something,
in approval or revulsion. Her manner, against my loud voice, ex-
asperated me. She sounded like an older sister to a kid brother, and
therefore stronger."[11]

Her letter to her husband, like other letters in Mphahlele's fiction,
is touching in its simple declaration of her position. It ends:

> . . . it horrifies me to think that you might have known when you married me
> that you were going to keep me as a wife for your country pleasure and keep
> a wife for your city pleasures one who knows how to smile for people in high
> places one who knows how to walk like white people one who takes out a
> handkerchief for everything that comes out of her face tears mucuous saliva
> so as not to remove the paint. If you wanted to keep me as a wife you love
> why did you do something you knew would hurt me would tear me apart?
> You are free to divorce me Chimba you should have felt free to do so long
> ago but at thirty-one I am prepared to go back to the Copperbelt with the
> children where I will find work to bring them up I do not want your money
> if you want to buy them anything or save it for them that is your own
> business for me you should not worry It is finished Your wife Tirenje.[12]

At first she seems undaunted by the trial, but as it progresses and
she witnesses the events she instigated cascading out of her reach,
we gradually see her disintegrate. She had brought the charge partly
to force Chirundu to come back to her and partly to make him give
up politics which first took him away from her. When she admits to
herself that neither will ever happen, she breaks down. From what
we know of her, however, and with the loving help of her husband's
nephew, we feel she will find herself again.

Except for Tirenje and Letanka, the characters seem to lack personality. Even Chirundu is hardly fascinating. Mphahlele does not
seem to be deeply involved with them as he was with the people in
The Wanderers. As a result they lack interest and tend to make the
novel dull. Lack of tension is aggravated by the method of narration.

Mphahlele again favors the vehicle of several narrators, presumably to show various points of view, but this time it leads to confusion. The novel begins with a conversation between the prisoners
and comes back to them several times in the form of dramatic

dialogues, at times reminiscent of the royal prisoner and his retinue in Wole Soyinka's *Kongi's Harvest*. Here, however, they merely comment on the action but contribute nothing new that the reader cannot gather for himself from the narrative. The trial scenes are dramatized, but even these lack dramatic interest. The first trial scene is followed by Chirundu's thoughts about it. He then goes on to narrate the events of his youth, switching backward and forward in place and time. From rambling thoughts this portion becomes a dramatic monologue and then a first-person narrative. The device is forced and clumsy and detracts from the realism of the action.

Later we hear the same story from Tirenje's point of view and then from Moyo's, neither of them contributing a great deal that is new. One feels at times that Mphahlele might originally have envisaged the work as a play, and indeed the discipline of the stage would have provided a better vehicle for the flashes of drama that the plot provides. Much that is unnecessary in the background and duplicated scenes would then have been cut and the confusing changes in time and place avoided.

Mphahlele's style has become simpler and more colloquial. The dialogue, however, is often as stilted as in his very early fiction, and the slick sophisticated slang does not always flow easily from his pen. Here is Pitso's comment on Chirundu's impending trial: ". . . Why would the blinking idiot go and legalize a city cunt when he could have access to it without all that paper and dotted line and ring stuff? The people who'll be looking on must think him an ass because they have extramural cunts all over the place while they play the dutiful husband and father. Why would the daffer do this kind of thing, why?"[13] Equally inadept is his description of a seductive woman. "Every movement of hers in the house, any time of day, seems to say to you, 'Come in, it's moist and vibrating for you.' "[14]

The autobiographical element has almost disappeared, yet we do get it here and there. Exile is still a painful experience which we can share with one of his characters. Pitso says: "— have you ever longed for your people so badly it seems to drain your blood? Leaves a dull ache here in the chest, like you're standing on the bank of a river that can't be crossed and they're standing on the other side beckoning you to come and they say *come, if you can't stay there 'cause we are not going to leave our homes.* Hell, man, it gives you an ache in your bowels you can't get used to or don't want to get used to."[15] Even Chirundu sometimes becomes Mphahlele's mouthpiece, as when he describes the past in African history and culture as being the servant of the present. Like Mphahlele, Chirundu was a teacher who resigned on a matter of principle and entered politics from a feeling of inevitability. Like Mphahlele, he rejects Christianity and stakes his faith in man.

The disappointment about the lack of welcome to refugees from South Africa is also something that Mphahlele felt personally. In *The Wanderers* he mentions black South Africans returning home from Zambia. Mphahlele lived in Zambia for almost two years and must have spent a great deal of time studying the country from various aspects. Like Letanka, he seems to have turned from his own discipline to history and displays an intimate knowledge of and pride in Africa's past.

This is Mphahlele's first truly African novel. He now accepts a background completely remote from the Christian-Western European townships of the Transvaal. The plot is based on the concept that polygamy, even if controversial, is psychologically and morally possible. In his earlier fiction characters had doubts about the church to which they belonged, but here he goes deeply into African religion and the effects of conversion to Christianity. The African's veneration of old age is clearly expressed and becomes a reality. Chirundu says:

Old age draws me to itself. You look at old age and you seem to be in the presence of an awful mystery. One that commands reverence and at the same time seems indifferent . . . He [an elderly man] is an ancestor now. Time has poured into this life all it could ever invest. This man, this woman you see in front of you in their seventies, eighties, nineties, has earned that status. In Europe and America, I've been told, they would be tucked away in a home, out of the concourse of general humanity. Or they would be confined in a private room in the house. Moyo would be seen as having towed behind him a wreckage for the scrapyard. To us, he would be walking beside a god. . . .[16]

The contrast between the dignity of the country and the corruption and superficiality of the city is also new in Mphahlele's fiction. It is personified by Chirundu's two women and appears again in a description of what happens after the death of Moyo's grandfather. The body is taken to a room with a concrete floor where it is hosed by a man who turns it over with a long stick. Moyo says: "I was burning with anger and disgust, so vulgar the whole business looked: that my grandfather should be handled like some animal at a slaughter house. Other corpses that waited in line went through the same treatment. The body was dried, dressed and taken to the grave." It would have been different, he says nostalgically, "back home."[17]

Starkly dramatic symbols are another innovation, though at times they appear Elizabethan rather than African. When cows come thundering into the homestead of Moyo's parents, the stampede marks a change in the family fortunes. Nsato, the python, is a portent of evil as well as a symbol of power. When it takes a woman in its coils it is a sign of dire change to come. As a power symbol it represents various aspects: sexual power, the power of destruction, and power that you face and measure so as to give you strength. This latter quality is explained by old Ambuye:

Everyone needs to know him — he is king, ancestor — you need to look at him a long time even though you are frightened — everyone has something he fears most — so much so his fart could kill a tribe of crocodiles — but when you have come face to face with the thing you dread most, or peep into its sleeping place and see it, that fear will make you strong — to know the size of sato is to know the size of your fear the size of your liver the size of the stone you need to swallow for the strength you need.[18]

Although completed early in 1974, "Chirundu" had not been accepted for publication at the time of writing. The reasons are open to speculation. *Down Second Avenue* found a ready market both for its intrinsic value and the general interest in the subject matter, which came as a revelation to its white readers. The same applies to most of the short stories. Mphahlele's critical works and essays were the product of a recognized scholar in his discipline. *The Wanderers*, dealing with the sublimated experiences of the exile, still has some of the evocative charisma of *Down Second Avenue*. "Chirundu," as part of an established Pan-African literature, must stand solely on its merit. It must stand comparison with the works of established African writers of the stature of Achebe, Soyinka, and others. As a result, publishers feel free to accept or reject. It is almost as though Mphahlele has entered an alien field as a newcomer and still has to find his way. Also at the time of writing, Mphahlele has turned to writing poetry. Some of his poems have appeared in periodicals, too recently to be included in this study. They are listed in the bibliography.

As a teacher Mphahlele continues to extend himself and to find fulfillment. "If I don't teach, I think I'll shrivel up into anonymity," he says in the essay "Why I Teach my Discipline." "I don't like anonymity. I'm a vain man, . . . I'm entertaining myself, which is also a process of self-education."[19]

Although he feels that he cannot make a contribution to American culture, yet he finds there "circles of human intercourse" sufficient to sustain him in exile, such as he feels he could find "nowhere else in the world (at any rate at this time) because Americans are all exiles of one kind or another." And he cherishes contact with students who acknowledge some impact he has made on them. As for his writing, if his contribution lies there, it is not for him, he says, to judge "what *that* legacy is worth."[20]

Conclusion

IT is for us, as his readers, to judge what the legacy of Mphahlele's writing is worth up to the present time. As for the future, his creative talent can probably gain its full potential only if he returns to South Africa and resumes his function of teaching his discipline in his own setting, and of encouraging the different elements in South Africa to combine and interchange in producing a modern indigenous literature. In this respect he does not regard the white man as alien to Africa, in the same way as does, for instance, Achebe in his writing. For Mphahlele, he is an established part of Africa; it is his present thought processes that are alien to the land.

For the present, Mphahlele remains, as he has always been, a lonely man, destined to think in isolation. Right from the beginning he was recognized as a writer, teacher, and spokesman, but he was never part of the current scene or movement. His colleagues on *Drum* respected him, but he was an outsider to their group. In his address to the Second Congress of Negro Writers and Artists in Rome[1] he describes the escape others found in jazz to fortify themselves for the next day's demands, for the hurts and insults from the white man, the long bus queues. He himself faced the situation soberly throughout his life. His work arises out of the anguish caused by these demands. Today he is recognized as the doyen of black South Africa writers, and the leading African critic, but his views are heavily criticized by those among whom he lives. In his own land his voice is silenced. In the essay "Tyranny of Place" he says that exiles like him will never know what the people think of them — those whose concerns they share in South Africa and who make the material for their writing.

Yet Mphahlele's voice does reach his homeland. There are few black teachers of English in South Africa, for instance, who have not heard of him and managed to obtain his writing. Whenever black

African literature is mentioned in South Africa, his name comes up. It would be an impossible task for libraries to eliminate every anthology and journal containing essays, short stories, and extracts of his longer works, as the law requires. Educational representatives from South Africa attend conferences abroad where they hear him speak or his work is discussed.

In the rest of Africa, in England, the United States, Sweden, and elsewhere, he is recognized as an important African writer and a leader in his field. As William Plomer said of him when reviewing *Down Second Avenue* for *The New Statesman,* "Respect for himself as a man and a writer he has already won. He is a participant in the great non-racial effort of winning the durable from the transient."[2]

This has been his main objective: to reproduce, grasp, and interpret what is essential and permanent in life and literature. A gentle man, he has turned his anguish and bitterness into an acceptance of a situation, not as one that he cannot change, but as an existing condition under which one can still find meaning in life. He has taught the younger writers that to know one's sorrow is to know one's joy.[3] He has worked toward a balance between artistic integrity and social involvement. He not only talks about this in his essays and lectures, but demonstrates it in his fiction and autobiographical works. These, at their best, succeed through their vibrancy in translating his concepts into a living art.

Notes and References

Preface

[Unless another author's name appears, all titles are by Mphahlele.]

1. African Scandinavian Writers' Conference, held at Hüselberg Castle outside Stockholm, February 6-9, 1967, under the auspices of the Scandinavian Institute of African Studies, The Swedish Institute for Cultural Relations with Foreign Countries, as reported by Per Wästberg in *Modern Africa* (New York: Africana Publishing Company, 1969).

2. Ezekiel Mphahlele, *Down Second Avenue* (London: Faber and Faber, 1959).

Chapter One

1. 2 March - 1 April, 1949.

2. "Negro Culture in a Multi-Racial Society in Africa," *Presence Africaine*, Special Issue, 24-25 February-May, 1959, 225.

3. *Down Second Avenue*, p. 11.

4. Ibid., p. 51.

5. "Why I Teach My Discipline," *Denver Quarterly* VIII, 1, 34.

6. "The Dilemma of the African Exile," *Twentieth Century*, April, 1959, p. 319.

7. "The Tyranny of Place," *New Letters*, XL, 1, 70.

8. Ian Munro, Reinhard Sander, Richard Priebe, "Excerpts from an Interview with the South African Writer Ezekiel Mphahlele," *Studies in Black Classics*, I, 1, 39.

9. *Down Second Avenue*, p. 164.

10. "The Tyranny of Place," 69.

11. Ibid., p. 81.

12. *Man Must Live and Other Stories* (Cape Town: The African Bookman, 1946), p. 50.

13. Ibid., p. 51.

14. Ibid., pp. 24 - 25.

15. Ibid., pp. 25 - 26.

16. "The African Intellectual," Prudence Smith, ed., *Africa in Transition*, Some BBC Talks on Changing Conditions in the Union and the Rhodesias (London: Max Reinhardt, 1958).

17. *Man Must Live*, p. 29.

18. Ibid., p. 4.

19. Ibid., pp. 7 - 8.

20. Ibid., p. 27.

21. Ibid., p. 23.

22. Ibid., p. 43.

23. Ibid., p. 40.

24. Ibid., p. 39.

25. Ibid., p. 42.

26. Ibid., p. 50.

27. *Down Second Avenue*, p. 217.

28. Ibid., p. 126.

29. Peter Abrahams, *Return to Goli* (London: Faber and Faber, 1953).

30. *Down Second Avenue*, p. 165.

31. Peter Abrahams, *Song of the City* (London: Dorothy Crisp, 1945).

32. Peter Abrahams, *Mine Boy* (London: Faber and Faber, 1946).

33. R. R. R. Dhlomo, *An African Tragedy* (Alice: Lovedale, undated).

34. *Man Must Live*, p. 1.

35. *Down Second Avenue*, p. 164.

Chapter Two

1. "Why I Teach My Discipline," p. 32.

2. "The Syllabus and the Child," *The Good Shepherd*, November, 1952, p. 7.

3. *Down Second Avenue*, p. 169.

4. "Black and White," *The New Statesman*, 10 September, 1960, p. 346.

5. Anthony Sampson, *Drum* (London: Collins, 1956), p. 15.

6. Ibid., p. 28.

7. *The African Image* (London: Faber and Faber, 1962), p. 97.

8. *The Wanderers*, (New York: MacMillan, 1971), p. 122.

9. Ibid., p. 127.

10. "The Tyranny of Place," *New Letters*, XL, 1, 77.

11. *The Wanderers*, p. 104.

12. "The Boycott that has Become a War," *Drum*, July, 1957, p. 19.

13. *Down Second Avenue*, p. 188.

14. Ibid., p. 188.

15. "The Real Africa," *Commonwealth Challenge*, VIII, 4, 54.

16. *African Image*, p. 37.

17. "Excerpts from an Interview with the South African Writer Ezekiel Mphahlele," 39. (See Note 8, Chapter 1.)

18. "Lesane," *Drum*, December, 1956.

19. Ibid., p. 43.
20. Ibid., p. 45.
21. "Lesane," *Drum*, February, 1957, p. 54.
22. *African Image*, p. 23.
23. *Down Second Avenue*, p. 59.
24. Bruno Ezekiel (pseud.), "Reef Train," *Drum*, August, 1954, p. 34.
25. "Down the Quiet Street," *Drum*, January, 1956, pp. 49 - 50.
26. "Across Down Stream," *Drum*, August, 1955. Later published as "The Coffee-Cart Girl." *In Corner B* (Nairobi: East African Publishing House, 1967).
27. "Mrs. Plum," *In Corner B*.
28. "Blind Alley," *Drum*, September, 1953.
29. "Lesane," *Drum*, December, 1956, p. 42.
30. Ibid., p. 54.
31. "Lesane," *Drum*, April, 1957, p. 47.
32. "Blind Alley," p. 32.
33. Peter Abrahams, *Tell Freedom* (London: Faber and Faber, 1954).
34. "Across Down Stream," p. 50.
35. Ibid., p. 50.
36. Ibid., p. 53
37. "Down the Quiet Street," p. 48.
38. "Lesane," *Drum*, December, 1956, p. 41.
39. Ibid., p. 45.
40. Ibid., p. 47.
41. "Lesane," *Drum*, February, 1957, p. 55.
42. "Lesane," March, 1957, p. 46.
43. "Lesane," April, 1957, p. 47.
44. "Lesane," January, 1957, p. 46.
45. "Lesane," April, 1957, p. 46.
46. "Lesane," January, 1957, p. 54.
47. Anthony Sampson, "Orlando Revisited," *Africa South*, III, 4, July-September, 1950, 44.
48. *The Wanderers*, p. 122.
49. *Down Second Avenue*, p. 49.
50. *The Wanderers*, p. 53.
51. *Down Second Avenue*, p. 200.
52. Ibid., p. 210.

Chapter Three

1. Bruce Mazlish, "Autobiography and Psychoanalysis," *Encounter*, October, 1970, p. 28.
2. *Down Second Avenue*, p. 184.
3. Ibid., p. 185.
4. Ibid., p. 153.

5. Dennis Duerden, ed., *African Writers Talking* (London, Ibadan, Nairobi: Heinemann, 1972). Cosmo Pieterse interviewing Ezekiel Mphahlele at the Transcription Centre, London, 1969.

6. Peter Abrahams, *Tell Freedom* (London: Faber and Faber, 1954), p. 9.

7. *Down Second Avenue*, p. 11.

8. Ibid., p. 111.

9. Ibid., p. 105.

10. Ibid., p. 42.

11. Ibid., pp. 71 - 72.

12. "The Woman," *The Purple Renoster*, Spring, 1957. Also in *The Living and Dead and Other Stories* (Ibadan: Ministry of Education, 1961).

13. "The Woman Walks Out," *Standpunte*, VIII, 4. Also in *The Living and Dead and Other Stories*.

14. *Down Second Avenue*, p. 74.

15. Ibid., p. 46.

16. Langston Hughes, ed., *An African Treasury* (London: Gollancz, 1961). Can Themba, "Requiem for Sophiatown," p. 11 et seq.

17. Bloke Modisane, *Blame Me on History* (London: Thames and Hudson, 1963).

18. "Requiem for Sophiatown," p. 10.

19. *Down Second Avenue*, p. 182.

20. Ibid., p. 43.

21. Ibid., p. 150.

22. Ibid., p. 39.

23. Ibid., p. 40.

24. Ibid., p. 18.

25. Ibid., p. 30.

26. Ibid., p. 39.

27. Ibid., pp. 29 - 30.

28. Lewis Nkosi, "Conversations with Ezekiel Mphahlele," *Africa Report*, July, 1964, pp. 8 - 9.

29. *Down Second Avenue*, p. 76.

30. Ibid., p. 78.

31. Ibid., p. 59.

32. Ibid., pp. 136 - 137.

33. Ibid., p. 174.

34. Janheinz Jahn, *Muntu*, translated by Marjorie Grene (London: Faber and Faber, 1958), pp. 211 - 212.

35. Anne Tibble, *African/English Literature, A Survey and Anthology* (London: Peter Owen, 1965), p. 46.

Chapter Four

1. "A South African in Nigeria," *Africa South*, III, July-September, 1959, 4, 99.

2. Ibid., 104.
3. *The Wanderers,* p. 174.
4. Ibid., p. 221.
5. *African Image,* p. 223.
6. Lewis Nkosi, "Conversation with Ezekiel Mphahlele," *African Report,* July, 1964.
7. *African Image,* revised edition (London: Faber and Faber, 1973). In future notes, *African Image* will refer to the original edition, *African Image* (revised) to the later edition.
8. "The Tyranny of Place," *New Letters,* XL, 1, 78.
9. Langston Hughes, ed., *An African Treasury* (London: Gollancz, 1960), "Accra Conference Diary," by Ezekiel Mphahlele, pp. 36 et seq.
10. Letter to the author.
11. *The Living and Dead and Other Stories* (Ibadan: Ministry of Education, 1961), p. 8.
12. Ibid., p. 17.
13. *African Image* (revised), p. 14.
14. Ibid., p. 126.
15. Ibid., p. 128.
16. Ibid., p. 130.
17. *African Image* (revised), p. 131.
18. *African Image,* p. 108.
19. *The Living and Dead,* p. 7.
20. Ibid., p. 14.
21. Ibid., p. 16.
22. Ibid., p. 17.
23. Ibid., p. 7.
24. Ibid., p. 21.
25. Ibid., p. 21.
26. Ibid., p. 30.
27. Ibid., p. 31.
28. Ibid., p. 36.
29. Ibid., p. 36.
30. Ibid., p. 41.
31. Ibid., p. 46.
32. Ibid., p. 47.
33. Ibid., p. 51.
34. Ibid., p. 54.
35. Ibid., p. 49.
36. Ibid., p. 52.
37. Ibid., p. 63.
38. Ibid., p. 64.
39. Ibid., p. 66.
40. Ibid., p. 65.

Chapter Five

1. *In Corner B* (Nairobi: East African Publishing House, 1967), p. 11.

2. *In Corner B*, p. 20.

3. Ibid., p. 15.

4. Ibid., p. 16.

5. Ibid., p. 20.

6. Ibid., p. 8.

7. Ibid., p. 7.

8. O. R. Dathorne and Willfried Feuser, eds., *Africa in Prose* (Harmondsworth: Penguin Books, 1969), p. 288.

9. *In Corner B*, p. 153.

10. Ibid., p. 154.

11. Ezekiel Mphahlele and Ellis Ayitey Komey, eds., *Modern African Stories* (London: Faber and Faber, 1964).

12. *In Corner B*, p. 38.

13. Ibid., p. 54.

14. Ibid., p. 61.

15. Ibid., p. 60.

16. Ibid., p. 44.

17. Ibid., p. 47.

18. Ibid., p. 52.

19. Ibid., p. 56.

20. Ibid., p. 61.

21. Ibid., p. 57.

22. Ibid., p. 60.

23. Ibid., p. 38.

24. Ibid., p. 40.

25. Ibid., p. 41.

26. Ibid., p. 45.

27. Ibid., p. 46.

28. Ibid., p. 66.

29. Ibid., pp. 66 - 67.

30. Ibid., pp. 68 - 69.

31. Ibid., p. 108.

32. Ibid., pp. 108 - 109.

33. Ibid., p. 111.

34. Ibid., p. 109.

35. Ibid., p. 110.

36. Ibid., p. 115.

37. Ibid., p. 116.

38. Ibid., pp. 116 - 117.

39. Ibid., p. 117.

40. Ibid., p. 118.

41. Ibid., p. 120.

42. Ibid., pp. 124 - 125.
43. Ibid., pp. 125 - 126.
44. Ibid., p. 126.
45. Ibid., p. 123.
46. Ibid., pp. 168 - 169.
47. Ibid., p. 170.
48. Ibid., p. 164.
49. Ibid., p. 208.
50. Ibid., pp. 174 - 175.
51. Ibid., p. 175.
52. Ibid., p. 184.
53. Ibid., p. 185.
54. Ibid., p. 186.
55. Ibid., p. 189.
56. Ibid., p. 190.
57. Ibid., p. 193.
58. Ibid., p. 196.
59. Ibid., p. 200.
60. Ibid., p. 201.
61. Ibid., p. 197.
62. Ibid., p. 206.
63. Ibid., p. 183.
64. Ibid., p. 206.
65. Ibid., p. 196.
66. Ibid., p. 200.
67. Ibid., p. 201.
68. Ibid., p. 208.
69. Ibid., p. 179.
70. Ibid., p. 193.
71. Letter to author.

Chapter Six

1. *The African Image*, (revised), (London: Faber and Faber, 1973), p. 6.
2. *African Image*, (revised), p. 15.
3. Ibid., p. 16.
4. Ibid., p. 77.
5. Ibid., p. 70.
6. Ibid., p. 94.
7. Ibid., p. 95.
8. *African Image*, p. 53.
9. Ibid., p. 193.
10. Ibid., p. 23.
11. *African Image*, (revised), p. 79.
12. Ibid., p. 88.

13. Ibid., p. 89.

14. Ibid., p. 102.

15. Ibid., p. 122.

16. Ibid., p. 49.

17. Ibid., p. 56.

18. Ibid., p. 42.

19. *African Image*, pp. 222 - 223.

20. *African Image*, (revised), p. 43.

21. *African Image*, p. 22.

22. Ibid., p. 116.

23. Ibid., p. 159.

24. Ibid., p. 106.

25. Ibid., pp. 120 - 121.

26. *African Image*, (revised), p. 10.

27. Ibid., p. 226.

28. Ibid., p. 196.

29. *African Image*, p. 176.

30. *African Image*, (revised), p. 237.

31. Ibid., p. 238.

32. Ibid., p. 239.

33. Cosmo Pieterse, ed., *Seven South African Poets* (London: Heinemann, 1971), "Waiting" by Arthur Nortje, p. 125.

34. *African Image*, (revised), p. 249.

35. Mphahlele acknowledges his quotations from Gwendolyn Brooks' *In the Mecca* (New York: Harper and Row, 1964 [sic]).   ).

36. *Voices in the Whirlwind and Other Essays* (New York: Hill and Wang, 1972), p. 150.

37. *Voices in the Whirlwind*, p. 9.

38. Ibid., p. 47.

39. Ibid., p. 2.

40. Ibid., p. 4.

41. Christopher Caudwell, *Illusion and Reality: A Study of the Sources of Poetry* (Delhi: People's Publishing House, 1956).

42. I. A. Richards, *Principles of Literary Criticism* (London: Routledge and Kegan Paul, 1949).

43. Laurence Lerner, *The Truest Poetry* (London: Hamish Hamilton, 1960).

44. *Voices in the Whirlwind*, p. 7.

45. Ibid., p. 69.

46. Ibid., p. 76.

47. Ibid., p. 77.

48. Ibid., p. 97.

49. "African Literature, What Tradition?" *Denver Quarterly*, II, 2.

50. *Voices in the Whirlwind*, p. 125.

51. Ibid., p. 144.

52. Ibid., p. 169.
53. Ibid., p. 187.
54. Ibid., p. 188.
55. Ibid., p. 194.
56. Ibid., p. 195.
57. "Why I Teach My Discipline," *Denver Quarterly*, VIII, 1, 35 - 36.
58. Ibid., 36.
59. Ibid., 38 - 39.
60. Ibid., 41 - 42.
61. Ibid., 34.
62. Ibid., 35.
63. Ibid., 38.
64. Ibid., 39.
65. "Langston Hughes," *Orpheus* 9, June, 1964. Also published in *Introduction to African Literature*, ed. by Ulli Beier (London: Longman Green and Co., 1967).
66. "The Real Africa," *Commonwealth Challenge*, VII, 4, 54.
67. "Black Literature at the University of Denver," *Research in African Literature*, III, 1, 72.
68. "Why I Teach My Discipline," 32.
69. *Down Second Avenue*, p. 221.
70. "Out of Africa," *Encounter*, April, 1960.
71. Dan Jacobson, "Out of Africa," *Encounter*, October, 1959.
72. Addison Gayle Jr., "Review of *Voices in the Whirlwind and Other Essays* by Ezekiel Mphahlele," *Blackworld*, July, 1973, p. 48.
73. "Ezekiel Mphahlele's Reply to Addison Gayle Jr.," *Blackworld*, January, 1973, p. 5.
74. Ezekiel Mphahlele and Ellis Ayitey Komey, eds., *Modern African Stories* (London: Faber and Faber, 1964), p. 10.
75. *Modern African Stories*, pp. 10 - 11.
76. Ibid., p. 11.
77. Ibid., p. 12.
78. *African Writing Today* (Harmondsworth: Penguin, 1967).

Chapter Seven

1. Dennis Duerden and Cosmo Pieterse, eds., *African Writers Talking* (London, Ibadan, and Nairobi: Heinemann, 1972).
2. Letter to the author.
3. Bernth Lindfors, Ian Munro, Richard Priebe, Reinhard Sander, "Interview with Ezekiel Mphahlele," *Palaver*, African and Afro-American Research Institute, Austin, Texas, 1972, p. 41.
4. *The Wanderers*, p. 10.
5. Ibid., p. 111.
6. Ibid., p. 22.

7. Ibid., p. 53.
8. Ibid., p. 147.
9. Ibid., p. 280.
10. Ibid., p. 286.
11. Ibid., p. 310.
12. Ibid., p. 311.
13. Ibid., p. 301.
14. Ibid., p. 308.
15. Ibid., p. 107.
16. Ibid., p. 174.
17. Ibid., p. 221.
18. Ibid., p. 264.
19. Ibid., p. 204.
20. Ibid., p. 155.
21. "Travels of an Extramural Donkey," *Transition*, III, 11, 46 - 50.
22. *The Wanderers*, p. 171.
23. "Interview with Ezekiel Mphahlele," *Palaver*, pp. 41 - 42.
24. Letter to the author.
25. *African Image*, (revised), p. 249.
26. *The Wanderers*, p. 267.
27. Ibid., p. 17.
28. Ibid., p. 79.
29. Ibid., p. 78.
30. Ibid., p. 143.
31. Ibid., p. 249.
32. Ibid., p. 242.
33. Ibid., p. 245.
34. Ibid., p. 302.
35. Ibid., p. 259.
36. Ibid., p. 236.
37. Ibid., p. 11.
38. Ibid., p. 49.
39. "Interview with Ezekiel Mphahlele," *Palaver*, p. 44.
40. *The Wanderers*, p. 132.
41. Ibid., p. 127.
42. Ibid., p. 129.
43. Ibid., pp. 213 - 214.
44. Ibid., p. 119.
45. Alfred Hutchinson, *Road to Ghana* (London: Gollancz, 1960).
46. Bessie Head, *When Rain Clouds Gather* (London: Gollancz, 1969).
47. *The Wanderers*, p. 166.
48. Ibid., p. 299.
49. Ibid., p. 142.
50. "*The Wanderers*, a Novel of Africa," *African Arts/Arts d'Afrique*, II, 2, 12 - 15, 59 - 61.

51. J. Povey, "Search for a Homeland," Review of *The Wanderers*, *African Studies Review*, XIV, 3, 494 - 497.

52. Barney C. McCartney, Review of *The Wanderers*, *East Africa Journal*, special issue, July, 1971, pp. 41 - 42.

Chapter Eight

1. "Chirundu," Manuscript of novel, p. 73.
2. Ibid., p. 77.
3. Ibid., p. 14.
4. Ibid., p. 258.
5. Ibid., p. 157.
6. Ibid., pp. 174 - 175.
7. Ibid., p. 44.
8. Ibid., p. 59.
9. Ibid., p. 20.
10. Ibid., p. 72.
11. Ibid., p. 71.
12. Ibid., p. 105.
13. Ibid., p. 56.
14. Ibid., p. 37.
15. Ibid., p. 113.
16. Ibid., pp. 88 - 89.
17. Ibid., pp. 242 - 243.
18. Ibid., p. 188.
19. "Why I Teach My Discipline," *Denver Quarterly*, VIII, 1, 42.
20. Ibid., 43.

Conclusion

1. "Negro Culture in a Multi-Racial Society in Africa," *Presence Africaine*, Special Issue, No. 24 - 25, February-May 1959, 225 - 227.

2. William Plomer, Review of *Down Second Avenue*, *New Statesman*, April 25, 1959, pp. 582 - 583.

3. *"To know our sorrow*
   Is to know our joy —"
Concluding lines of stanza referring to Ezekiel Mphahlele in poem "For Zeke and Dennis," by Keorapetse Kgositsile, Bernth Lindfors, ed., *South African Voices* (Austin, Texas: African and Afro-American Studies and Research Center, 1975), p. 2.

Selected Bibliography

PRIMARY SOURCES

(arranged chronologically)

1. Books and Pamphlets written or edited by Ezekiel Mphahlele
Man Must Live and Other Stories. Cape Town: African Bookman, 1947; Ibadan: Ministry of Education, 1958.
Down Second Avenue. London: Faber and Faber, 1959; New York: Doubleday, 1971.
The Living and Dead and Other Stories. Ibadan: Ministry of Education, 1961.
The African Image. London: Faber and Faber, 1962; New York: Praeger, 1962, Revised edition; London: Faber and Faber, 1973.
Modern African Stories. Edited with Ellis Ayitey Komey. London: Faber and Faber, 1964.
A Guide to Creative Writing. Dar-es-Salaam, Nairobi, Kampala: East African Literature Bureau, 1966.
In Corner B. Nairobi: East African Publishing House, 1967.
African Writing Today. Edited. Harmondsworth: Penguin, 1967.
The Wanderers. New York: MacMillan, 1970.
Voices in the Whirlwind and Other Essays. New York: Hill and Wang, 1972.

2. Uncollected Short Stories
"Blind Alley." *Drum*, September, 1953, pp. 32 - 34.
"Reef Train." By Bruno Eseki (pseud.). *Drum*, August, 1954, pp. 34 - 35.
"Across Down Stream." By Bruno Eseki (pseud.). *Drum*, August, 1955, pp. 50 - 53. (Later published as "The Coffee-Cart Girl" in *In Corner B* — see above.)
"Down the Quiet Street." *Drum*, January, 1956, pp. 48 - 51.
"Lesane." *Drum*, December, 1956, pp. 41 - 49; January, 1957, pp. 60 - 67; February, 1957, pp. 53 - 55; March, 1957, pp. 45 - 49; April, 1957, pp. 42 - 47.

3. Uncollected Essays

"The Syllabus and the Child." *The Good Shepherd*, November, 1952, p. 7.

"The Boycott That Has Become a War." *Drum*, July, 1956, pp. 19 - 23.

"The Evaton Riots." *Africa South*, January-March, 1957, pp. 55 - 63.

"The African Intellectual." *Africa in Transition*, ed. Prudence Smith, pp. 149 - 158. London: Max Reinhardt, 1958.

"The Dilemma of the African Elite." *Twentieth Century*, April, 1959, pp. 319 - 325.

"Negro Culture in a Multi-Racial Society." *Présence Africaine*, special issue, 24 - 25 (February-May, 1959), pp. 225 - 227.

"The Real Africa." *Commonwealth Challenge*, VII, 4, (July, 1959), 53 - 54.

"A South African in Nigeria." *African South*, III, 4, (July-September, 1959), 99 - 104.

"Accra Conference." *An African Treasury*, ed. Langston Hughes, pp. 36 - 41. New York: Crown, 1960.

"The Function of Literature at the Present Time: The Ethnic Imperative." *Transition*, 45, IX, 2 (1974), 47 - 53.

"Out of Africa." *Encounter*, April, 1960, pp. 61 - 63.

"Black and White." *The New Statesman*, September 10, 1960, pp. 342 - 346.

"The Cult of Negritude." *Encounter*, March, 1961, pp. 50 - 52.

"Travels on an Extramural Donkey." *Transition*, III, 11, (November, 1963), 46 - 50.

"African Literature, What Tradition?" *Denver Quarterly*, II, 2 (Summer 1967), 36 - 68.

"Langston Hughes." *Orpheus*, I, 9, (June, 1964), 16 - 21.

"Chemchemi Centre, Nairobi." *Journal of Modern African Studies*, III, 1, (1965), 115 - 117.

"Black Literature at the University of Denver." *Research in African Literatures*, III, 1, (Spring 1972), 70 - 74.

"Remarks on Negritude." *African Writing Today*, ed. Ezekiel Mphahlele. Harmondsworth: Penguin, 1967.

"Why I Teach my Discipline." *Denver Quarterly*, VIII, 1, (Spring 1973), 32 - 43.

"The Tyranny of Place." *New Letters*. 40, 1 (1974), 69 - 84.

"Reply to Addison Gayle, Jr." *Blackworld*, January, 1974, pp. 4 - 20.

4. Theses

"The Non-European Character in South African English Fiction." Submitted to satisfy requirements for the degree of Master of Arts in the Department of English, University of South Africa, December, 1956.

"The Wanderers." Novel accepted as Ph.D. dissertation by University of California, June, 1968.

5. Manuscript

"Chirundu." A novel, completed 1974, unpublished.

6. Poems

"The Immigrant." *Black Orpheus*, November, 1959, pp. 23 - 27.

"Exile in Nigeria." *Poems from Black Africa*, ed. Langston Hughes, pp. 116 - 122. Bloomington and London: Indiana University Press, 1963.

"Death." *New African Literature and the Arts I*, ed. Joseph Okpaku, pp. 144 - 147. New York: Crowell, in association with Third World Press, 1970.

"Somewhere." *New African Literature and the Arts I*, ed. Joseph Okpaku, pp. 147 - 148. New York: Crowell, in association with Third World Press, 1970.

"Homeward Bound." *New African Literature and the Arts I*, ed. Joseph Okpaku, pp. 149 - 150. New York: Crowell, in association with Third World Press, 1970.

"Death II." *The Gar*, IV, 4 (March-April 1975), 14.

"Death III." *South African Voices*, ed. Bernth Lindfors, p. 26. Austin, Texas: African and Afro-American Studies and Research Center, 1975.

"A Poem for all the Victims of Tyranny in Southern Africa." *South African Voices*, ed. Bernth Lindfors, p. 26. Austin, Texas: African and Afro-American Studies and Research Center, 1975.

SECONDARY SOURCES

(arranged alphabetically)

1. Books

ABRAHAMS, PETER. *Song of the City*. London: Dorothy Crisp, 1945.

———. *Mine Boy*. London: Faber and Faber, 1946.

———. *Return to Goli*. London: Faber and Faber, 1953.

———. *Tell Freedom*. London: Faber and Faber, 1954.

BEIER, ULLI, ed. *Introduction to African Literature*. London: Longman, 1967.

CARTEY, WILFRED. *Whispers from a Continent*. New York: Random House, 1969.

DATHORNE, O. R., and FEUSER, WILLFRIED, eds. *Africa in Prose*. Harmondsworth: Penguin, 1969.

DHLOMO, R. R. R. *An African Tragedy*. Alice: Lovedale, undated.

DUERDEN, DENNIS, ed. *African Writers Talking*. London, Ibadan, and Nairobi: Heinemann, 1972.

GORDIMER, NADINE, and ABRAHAMS, LIONEL. *South African Writing Today*. Harmondsworth: Penguin, 1967.

HEAD, BESSIE. *When Rain Clouds Gather*. London: Gollancz, 1969.

HOPKINSON, TOM. *In the Fiery Continent*. London: Gollancz, 1962.

HUGHES, LANGSTON, ed. *An African Treasury*. London: Gollancz, 1961.

———, ed. *Poems from Black Africa*. Bloomington and London: Indiana University Press, 1963.

HUTCHINSON, ALFRED. *Road to Ghana*. London: Gollancz, 1960.

JAHN, JANHEINZ. *Muntu*. London: Faber and Faber, 1958.

LINDFORS, BERNTH, ed. *South African Voices*. Austin, Texas: African and Afro-American Studies Center, 1975.

MODISANE, BLOKE. *Blame Me on History*. London: Thames and Hudson, 1963.

MOORE, GERALD. *Seven African Writers*. Oxford: Oxford University Press, 1962, reprinted with corrections, 1966.

NKOSI, LEWIS. *Home and Exile*. London and Ibadan: Longman, 1965.

OKPAKU, JOSEPH, ed. *New African Literature and the Arts I*. New York: Crowell, in association with Third World Press, 1970.

PIETERSE, COSMO, ed. *Seven South African Poets*. London: Heinemann, 1971.

SAMPSON, ANTHONY. *Drum*. London: Collins, 1956.

TIBBLE, ANNE. *African/English Literature, A Survey and Anthology*. London: Peter Owen, 1965.

2. Essays and Reviews

CREIGHTON, T. R. M. Review of *The African Image*. *Modern African Studies*, I, 1, (March, 1963), 117 - 118.

GAYLE, ADDISON, Jr. Review of *Voices in the Whirlwind and Other Essays*. *Blackworld*, July, 1973, pp. 40 - 48.

GORDIMER, NADINE. "Censored, Banned, Gagged." *Encounter*, June, 1963, pp. 59 - 63.

———. "Towards a Desk-Drawer Literature." *The Classic*, II, 4 (1968), 64 - 74.

———. "The Novel and the Nation." *Times Literary Supplement*, August 11, 1961, pp. 520 - 523.

JACOBSON, DAN. "Out of Africa." *Encounter*, October, 1959, pp. 68 - 71.

LINDFORS, BERNTH; MUNRO, IAN; PRIEBE, RICHARD; and SANDER, REINHARD. "Interview with Ezekiel Mphahlele." *Palaver*, pp. 39 - 44. Austin, Texas: African and Afro-American Research Institute, 1972.

MCCARTNEY, BARNEY C. Review of *The Wanderers*. *East Africa Journal*, Special Issue, July, 1971, pp. 41 - 42.

MUNRO, IAN; SANDER, REINHARD; and PRIEBE, RICHARD. "Excerpts from and Interview with the South African writer Ezekiel Mphahlele." *Studies in Black Classics*, I, 1, 39 - 41.

NKOSI, LEWIS. "Conversations with Ezekiel Mphahlele." *Africa Report*, July, 1964, pp. 8 - 9.

PLOMER, WILLIAM. Review of *Down Second Avenue*. *New Statesman*, April 25, 1959, pp. 582 - 583.

POVEY, J. "Search for a Homeland." *African Studies Review*, XIV, 3, 494 - 497.

SAMPSON, ANTHONY. "Orlando Revisited." *Africa South*, July-September, 1959, pp. 40 - 44.

Index

191